WOMEN'S MONEY MATTERS

YOUR GUIDE TO FINANCIAL SECURITY

Diane K. Keister, CFP, ChFC

Certified Financial Planner
Chartered Financial Consultant

CUSTOM PUBLISHING

60 FIFTH AVE · NEW YORK, NY · 10011

NEW YORK · CHICAGO · WASHINGTON D.C. · LOS ANGELES · TORONTO

The views and opinions expressed in this book are solely those of the author and have not been approved or reviewed by her employer.

This book is designed to provide accurate and authoritative information in regard to the subject matter covered. It is sold with the understanding that prior to implementing any financial plans, the services of a competent professional should be sought. The use of this book is not a substitute for legal, accounting, or other professional services.

Investment decisions have certain inherent risk. Any investments a reader may make based on this information is at the reader's risk.

For information contact:
Diane K. Keister, CFP, ChFC
Financial Achievement Resources
11988 Charter House Lane
St. Louis, MO 63146
(314) 567–1384 or toll-free (877) 454–9397

CIP Data is available.
Printed in the United States of America
10 9 8 7 6 5 4 3 2 1

ISBN 0–8281–1311–4

DEDICATION

TO MY HUSBAND, DAVID, FOR BEING HUMOROUS AND LOVING. ESPECIALLY FOR HIS WORDS OF ENCOURAGEMENT AND INSPIRING CONTRIBUTIONS.

Thanks, also, to the hundreds of women who completed surveys,
spent time talking with me during my research and offered many helpful suggestions.

**WORKING CREATES INCOME.
INVESTMENTS CREATE WEALTH.**

—DIANE K. KEISTER

TABLE OF CONTENTS

INTRODUCTION

How does one go about writing a book to help women learn more about investing? After spending about 14 years in the financial arena, in banking and tax preparation, insurance and real estate, I found a reality that perplexed me. Many more men than women seemed to take "control" of their investment dollars. Whether single, in a relationship of marriage, or simply with a significant other, the male gender somehow thought that investing was their exclusive domain. Why this was? After all, women are every bit as intelligent!

I surveyed hundreds of women from all walks of life. Women with a diversity of backgrounds, from a snake charmer to the CEO of a Fortune 500 company. From an archeologist to a NASA astronaut. From a stay-at-home mom to the first lady of the State of Wisconsin. Their ages ranged from 17–96. Yes, 96 years old. Although she could have told me she was 76 and I would have believed her. I hope I'm in that good of shape, both mentally and physically (she still goes bowling once a week), when I'm 96. She has traveled the world, twice. She is one of the most interesting people I've ever met. There were also many cultures represented as well as women from each of the four relationship scenarios (single, married, divorced and widowed).

Many of the women I spoke with have lived through several of these relationship scenarios and had extremely dramatic, sometimes very sad, stories to tell. These women are doctors, school teachers, attorneys, secretaries, nurses, business owners, college professors, welders, office managers, computer programmers, electricians, real estate brokers, librarians and executives directors of non-profit organizations. As I spoke with more and more women, I realized just how important the subject of investing is. Something else I discovered is that there are not enough, not nearly enough, books that discuss the special needs of the female gender.

Some of the information, however, was surprising. Women don't want a "women's" investment plan. Women simply want, like their male counterparts, the information necessary to make informed decisions based on their personal financial needs and goals. What came through loud and clear, in almost every survey, was the fact that women recognize that they are going to be faced with certain financial situations that men are not.

Over the past several generations, women have steadily climbed the ladder of success. Today, growing numbers of women have reached unprecedented milestones in the world of business and beyond. According to the National Foundation for Women Business Owners, women-owned companies numbered 7.9 million in 1996, an 18% increase since 1990, and generated nearly $2.3 trillion in sales while employing over 18.5 million people. Women are going to college in greater numbers than men today, and are starting businesses at twice the rate of men.

By the year 2000, an estimated 50% of all businesses in this county will be women-owned. Currently, women-owned businesses in North America employ more people than all the Fortune 500 companies worldwide.

Women we are earning more money and creating more wealth than ever before. According to U.S. Census figures, American women collectively earn over a trillion dollars a year, up from $202 billion in 1975. There are 58 million women in the American work force and we continue to gain greater monetary power and influence. According to the IRS, nearly 43% of households with assets of $500,000 or more are headed by women. Even at the level of household assets of $600,000, 42% are still headed by women.

Since the early 1980s, women have been the fastest growing segment of the work force. Many women are managing their own finances by becoming active, educated investors. More and more women are laying the groundwork for their financial futures. With all of this extraordinary information, one might think that all is rosy. Yes, it is true that many great changes have come about because of our gender, but this has not come without a great deal of hard work and many, many sacrifices. Nearly 9 out of 10 women will be forced to make financial decisions alone as a result of divorce or widowhood. Today, $3/4$ of our senior citizens living in poverty are still women and the average woman can expect to spend more years caring for her elderly parents than for her own children.

Of all the troubling issues we face in this day and age, there are few that concern me as much as the financial future of women. This may seem like a strange concern after all the positive information at hand. But for all the progress we've made, there's still a long way to go. The way we live today, being so different from previous generations, has made it more important than ever for women to face financial responsibilities right now! Because I feel so strongly about this critical issue for women and their families, I have spent countless hours asking the questions that needed to be asked. This research has revealed that women do have a strong desire to learn more about investing and to gain more control over their financial security.

I have written this book because I feel that, next to your physical health, the single most important factor influencing your future happiness is your financial well-being. One last thing . . . I promise that taking control of your future financial security is easier than you think!

"The greatest mistake any woman can make is being financially unprepared."

—*Diane K. Keister*

INSPIRING WOMEN IN HISTORY

1

Throughout history there have been many great women. In researching for this book, I discovered that very little is known about some of the most influential women, our first ladies. I also discovered that it is not unusual for there to be no written records of a woman's life prior to the nineteenth century.

Several factors have made women much less visible than men in our nation's history. For most of the nation's past, "history" was defined as the lives and deeds of great men whose activities took place in the world of military, economic, or public life. Presidents, politicians, and generals; wars, battles, or major economic changes were what historians (mostly men) wrote about. The details of women's lives—their homes and families, their work in helping their husbands succeed in farming, business, or a career—often were not kept or considered important enough to record.

Historians tend to rely on written records, which many women did not leave. In the early days of the nation it was generally thought unimportant to educate women, and some never learned to read or write. At a time when the nation was more agricultural and rural, and most women married and raised families, education for daughters was not as important as it was for sons, who conducted the family's business.

When women did leave information about themselves in writing, they kept records in an informal way, through letters, diaries, and recipe and medical treatment books. While such documents were often considered important sources of information about men—because men most frequently wrote about public life—they were not considered valid in the same way for women. Stories of the family passed on by descendants, called oral or spoken history, were another form of recording events used by women. Until recently most historians didn't consider oral histories worth recording either. And if the lives of most white, middle-class women were thought of as not significant enough for history, the lives of African-American and Native American women, as well as immigrant women, were pushed even more to the side.

Because first ladies were married to presidents, who were powerful and influential men, I found that their letters and papers have been preserved as part of the family's history. But it was even hard to find information about some of the early first ladies—either because they didn't write many letters or keep a diary, or because their descendants didn't save them. Martha Washington, who had little formal education, was always embarrassed by her writing and spelling. She often told George what she wanted to say in a letter and he would write it for her. She would then copy it over in her own handwriting. After her husband died, Martha Washington burned their personal letters to each other, perhaps to protect her privacy. As a result, little is known about their personal life together.

In 1920, when women gained the vote, optimists hoped that this would begin a period of unprecedented progress for women in politics, business and society. But the people who came together in the suffrage campaign had many different views about the kinds of lives women should lead. As the boom years of the twenties gave way to the Great Depression of the Thirties, women's rights took second place to the very survival of the nation. Still, as America coped with the problems of Depression and then a Second World War, some women found new opportunities. They set examples that their daughters and granddaughters looked back to with pride when a new round of human rights struggles began in the sixties.

The Great Depression, which began in 1929 and lasted until the beginning of World War II, around 1940, *was in many ways a setback for women*. As employment rose, women were forced out of jobs. Men, people argued, needed to work to support their families. Women were falsely accused of holding jobs merely to buy frivolous items. At the same time, the difficulty of daily life made people focus on family and survival, not broad questions about women and society. In the Roosevelt administration, though, women made new gains when Frances Perkins was named Secretary of Labor, the first women to hold a cabinet post. Eleanor Roosevelt held her own press conferences at the White House, the first first lady to do so. Though African-American women held the lowest-paying job gained little support from the federal government, they gained an advocate in Washington through activist Mary McLeod Bethune's ties to Mrs. Roosevelt.

World War II, beginning for the United States with the bombing of Pearl Harbor in December 1941, brought dramatic changes in women's lives. As hundreds of thousands of men went to war, women were actively recruited to take their places. Advertisements appealed to women to enter jobs formerly open only to men and stressed the importance of their work to the war effort. Child-care centers were set up across the country to care for the children of working mothers at the same time as the All American Girls Professional Baseball Association gave women their first opportunity to compete as professionals in the "national pastime." Though the league was formed to make money, it served as a symbol of possibilities open to women during the war.

After the war, many of these opportunities disappeared. Government, business, and even labor unions urged women to return to the home to make way for the men returning from war. Having survived the Depression and then World War II, many Americans were eager to create secure, prosperous, and conventional lives. In the postwar prosperity, cars, homes, and household appliances were built in record numbers. ***Women were encouraged to be housewives, mothers, and consumers.*** Movies, novels, women's magazines, advertising, popular songs, and the new medium of television all stressed the importance of femininity and motherhood, at least for white women.

Yet, World War II had been a struggle against the worst of human tyranny, and after the war the barriers between men and women, and between blacks and whites, became harder to defend. After President Truman desegregated the armed forces in 1948, pressure to integrate all of America began to grow. As African-Americans fought for their rights in the 1950s and 1960s, they set a precedent women were eager to follow.

Inspired by Dr. Martin Luther King, Jr. and other civil rights leaders, college students, ministers, and thousands of others demonstrated and lobbied for the passage of the Civil Rights Act in 1964 and the Voting Rights Act in 1965. Finally, the rights African Americans had been granted after the Civil War were actively protected by the government. The experience of the civil rights struggle, combined with the protest movement against American involvement in Vietnam, encouraged a generation of Americans to question many of the established rules and social norms of their nation. One of their main targets was the restricted role of American women.

Betty Friedan wrote *The Feminine Mystique* **in 1963**, arguing that a woman need not be only a housewife and mother, but also should have access to other ways of expressing herself—in education, in work, in politics, in society. The book had a profound impact, and Friedan and other women launched the new women's rights movement in the mid-1960s. They formed the National Organization of Women (NOW) in 1966 to work for equality for women in every aspect of society. Women demanded the Equal Rights Amendment (ERA) be passed by Congress. They wanted equal pay for equal work and equal access to education, jobs, sports, and the military.

In the early 1970s, women successfully lobbied Congress to pass the ERA and send it to the states for ratification. They formed the National Women's Political Caucus to develop an agenda to elect more women to political office and to put women's issues at the center of political concerns. The Women's Equity Action League and the Women's Legal Defense Fund brought legal challenges to discrimination against women. Despite laws passed to provide more equal pay, in the 1970s women still earned only fifty-five cents for every dollar that men earned. Yet women gained entry into many areas of employment formerly closed to them, successfully ended quotas limiting women's acceptance to medical schools and law schools, and entered the professions in ever-increasing numbers. Indeed, in the seventies, college attendance by women surpassed that of men. In 1976, Barbara Walters became the first female journalist to hit the seven figure mark when she signed her $1-million dollar contract with ABC television.

By 1977, conservative women, led by Phyllis Schlafly and her organization the Eagle Forum, had organized across the country to defeat the ERA and other reforms that they believed would damage the home and family and bring to an end the "traditional" role of women. They raised fears among many that equality would make women just like men, undermine laws supporting marriage, end men's financial support of wives and children, force women into military combat, and make men and women share the same public bathroom facilities. While no one could prove these things would happen—in fact, many legal opinions said they would not—enough states voted against ratification to defeat the ERA in 1982.

The Reagan administration, beginning in 1981, swept into the White House on a wave of conservative support that continued during the Bush administration. The Republican party, which had supported the ERA since it was first introduced in 1923, dropped its support. Civil rights and women's equal access to work, pay, and education lost support.

On the other hand, on Wall Street, in law firms, in business schools and other graduate programs, and in the arts and the media, women became ever more prominent. While Geraldine Ferraro's pioneering campaign for the Vice Presidency in 1984 was unsuccessful, in the 1990s both parties scrambled to find female candidates and to appeal to the now-crucial female vote.

In the 1990s women were coming on strong in many areas. In 1992, Charlotte Beers is named chairman and CEO of Ogilvy & Mather ad agency; the percentage of female engineers inches up to 8.5 percent from 6.9 percent five years before, and race car driver Lyn St. James is named "Rookie of the Year" at the Indianapolis 500. Women continue to work toward pay equality, equal education, equal access to jobs, and greater representation in state legislatures and Congress. Also in 1992, and for the first time in our history, two women—Diane Feinstein and Barbara Boxer—were elected as senators from California. 1993 brought the passing of the Family and Medical Leave Act, which guaranteed an unpaid leave to anyone who needs to take care of a new infant or ill family member, and take our daughters to work day. By 1994, when Ann M. Fudge was promoted to president of Maxwell House Coffee, the number of women-owned businesses hiring workers was twice the rate of all U.S. businesses and 8 percent of Fortune 500 companies had at least one female director. In 1996, Madeline K. Albright became the first woman named Secretary of State, the highest-ranking position a woman has ever held in the Federal Government. In the same year Congress agrees to move the monument to early suffragists out of the Capitol basement and into the Rotunda. Remarkably, by 1996, Charlotte Beer led the most impressive turnaround of an ad agency at Ogilvy & Mather Worldwide, and was featured on the August 5, 1996 cover of Fortune magazine. After three different careers, in broadcast journalism, banking, and public service, Aida Alvarez was appointed head of the U.S. Small Business Administration (SBA) in early 1997.

This new female elite is definitely not your parents' paradigm. Not too long ago, executive women were overwhelmingly single and childless. They had to downplay their "sex appeal" and seemed insistent on being judged like men.

In the past twenty-five years or so (especially the last 10), a new field of women's history has emerged and grown in importance. Less formal sources for recording history, such as diaries, letters and oral history, have become significant in learning about women's lives. Work in the home, family history, changes in birthrate, and women's activities in formal politics have caught the interest of historians of both genders. Women historians in particular have helped people understand the role women have played in the building of our nation, and women's contributions are being recognized and given the value they deserve.

Today, women are becoming more and more visible in history and are entering government, politics, business and the professions as never before. In fact, as I write this in September of 1998, I am amazed and thrilled with the amount of money American businesswomen control and the power they wield. In fact, a new national survey called "Paths to Entrepreneurship," released in February 1998, was a report by the National Foundation for Women Business Owners (NFWBO), Catalyst, and the Committee of 2000. It set out to answer some questions:

Why are women becoming entrepreneurs in such unprecedented numbers and how do their experiences compare with those of their male counterparts? The study, funded by Salomon Smith Barney (one of the many global giants now marketing their services to women business owners), examined a random national sample of 800 businesses owned by men and women. The results challenge a number of old notions. While 16 percent of women entrepreneurs cited glass ceiling as a motivator for self-employment, more than 40 percent say they struck out on their own not because they didn't have opportunity, but because they felt bored and stifled by the corporate milieu. They were making it—on Wall Street, in law firms, at big companies—but they simply didn't feel their employers were giving them enough freedom to realize ambitions.

In the past decade, according to NFWBO, the number of women-owned businesses has skyrocketed by 78 percent (to an astounding 8 million); the number of people they employ has increased by 183 percent. Today, women provide jobs for one out of every four workers at American companies. The increase of women-owned firms is nearly twice the national rate.

Another important discovery: **Female entrepreneurs are better educated and more experienced than ever before.** Today's women business owners are more likely to have an MBA and high-level managerial experience than their predecessors. Before starting their own firms, 29 percent of women in business for 20 years or more did clerical work; that's true of only 8 percent of women in business for 10 years.

And it's no surprise that female entrepreneurs are also better capitalized. We've all heard the stories of women who maxed out their credit cards to start companies. But from 1992 to 1996, women's use of credit cards to fund new ventures dropped from 52 percent to 23 percent. Not only are women more savvy about getting funding, but there's also more money available. The 1992 NFWBO study that first brought to light the huge numbers of female small-business owners forced many big banks to reevaluate how they treated their women clients. Rather than view women as a poor credit risk, banks began to see an untapped market. In May of 1995, Wells Fargo Bank decided to lend $1 billion to women in small businesses and estimated that the money would be gone within four years. By the end of the first year, all the money had been handed out, and in 1996 the bank created a new $10 billion fund to support the demand. By the year 2000, women will control 40 to 50 percent of all companies in America. The current explosion already accounts for nearly $2.3 trillion in sales and 36 percent of all businesses.

Yes, we have come a long way, Baby! But there is still plenty of room not only at the top, but anywhere you'd like it to be! I think we can all be "Inspired Women" if we just allow ourselves to gain the knowledge necessary to tackle any situation. By picking this book you have decided to gain better control of your financial future. Continue reading and let me show you how to do just that.

SO, WHAT FINANCIAL CHALLENGES DO WOMEN FACE?

2

Investing is important for everyone—women and men. But there are a number of considerations that require a woman's close attention as we navigate our way to investment success. Burgeoning financial power isn't the only reason that women are becoming more active investors. Chances are good (80–90%) that nearly all women will be the sole guardian of their family's finances sometime in their lives. In addition, according to the American Institute of Economic Information, women often face financial situations that are specific to their gender:

* Women face more inflationary pressures because they live, on average, 7 years longer than men (a woman's life expectancy, from birth, is 78.3 years. A man's is only 71.5).

* 73% of females alive today will reach age 85 and 50% will reach age 90

* 44 percent of all marriages (that's 17 million women on average annually) end in divorce, according to 1997 year-end figures. The good news is that the number is down from 50% in both 1996 and 1995.

* Female headed households have increased 125% since 1960.

* 15% of U.S. households are women living alone vs. 8.7% in 1960.

* Today, women marry later in life than in any other time during history.

* The average age of widowhood is 55 (this may seem low, but for every woman in her late 60s who loses her husband, there is another in her 30s or 40s who suddenly finds herself alone).

* Half of all women older than 65 will out-live their husbands by 15 years.

The Journal of Population Economics shows that right after a woman goes through a divorce, her median income drops as much as 39%, while the average decline for men is 14%. It is not unusual for me to meet a woman in her late 50s, for example, who has to support herself, but she faces an extremely difficult time finding a job. For younger women, however, the income gap is less due to higher education levels. A look at statistics that shape our nation from the Census Bureau shows that young women narrow the wage gap but older women still face a greater discrepancy:

Women age 15–24 earn 95.5 cents for every dollar of a man's wage

Women age 25–34 earn 84.1 cents for every dollar of a man's wage

Women age 35–44 earn 71.8 cents for every dollar of a man's wage

Women age 45–54 earn 61.5 cents for every dollar of a man's wage

Women age 55–64 earn 63.2 cents for every dollar of a man's wage

Women age 65+ earn 67.1 cents for every dollar of a man's wage

Many women are at a distinct disadvantage in terms of their retirement savings as well. 80% of retired women have no pension benefits. Studies show that many women delay planning for retirement. A 1993 Merrill Lynch survey found that at age 40, only 40% of women respondents had started a retirement savings program. In the 45–64 age bracket, only 39% said they were saving for retirement. Think of yourself. Do you have your retirement plan prepared? Don't worry, you will after you finish this book.

Incidentally, women aren't alone in their lack of preparation for retirement. A new Gallop study commissioned by the New York Life Company found that professional men and women are "shockingly ill-informed" about retirement planning. Of those polled, 72% of the women and 53% of the men were "vaguely familiar or not at all familiar" with fundamental investing concepts like compounding, inflation, and tax-deferral. Also, a *Money Magazine* poll showed that nearly as many people have purchased lottery tickets for retirement (39%) as have invested in stocks (43%).

Social Security will not be much help, either. According to the National Center for Women and Retirement Research, although more women are becoming financially independent, less than 50% of those who are working have a current pension plan. In 1996, the average Social Security benefit pay to women was less than half that received by men. To meet the demands of raising a family and caring for relatives, many women take several years off from working—accounting for another hit to retirement savings. Divorce and widowhood pose additional challenges for female investors. As I stated earlier, there are 17 million divorced women in America, and in many cases these "suddenly single" women are left with limited financial resources. More detailed information about Social Security will follow in a later chapter.

Because you have picked this book, it shows that you are trying to gain all the investment knowledge you can to make wise financial decisions. "Women are generally doing a better job of investing than men," according to Thomas E. O'Hara (yes, a man) of the National Association of Investors, Corp., a federation of independent investment clubs. O'Hara reports that all-women investment clubs have historically gotten returns at least one full percentage point ahead of all-men clubs. However, the women involved in investment clubs are the exception. Research shows that most women tend to be overly conservative with their investments and generally don't invest enough in equities (stocks). Yet, given the financial challenges women face, such as longer life expectancy and lower retirement income, it's vital that they put enough into investments that provide growth.

GO AHEAD! PITCH THE JUNK AND GET ORGANIZED

3

You know it's there somewhere. Your passport, that is. And the 1997 year-end brokerage statement your accountant has been asking for ever since April 15th, when she filed the extension to your tax return. But if 15 minutes of scratching your head and rifling through an overstuffed file cabinet doesn't help locate such documents, take heart. You're not alone. Your personal files, like those of many people, are crying for a make over.

Some people are so disorganized that they arrive at their accountants or financial planners with mounds of important financial papers in shoe boxes and shopping bags. I once had a client come into my office with a laundry basket full of papers. She said, "Here's my life. Fix it!" Another elderly woman client, who had lost her husband about 5 months earlier, came in and said, "Do you remember when you told me to go through all the stuff in the basement and attic as soon as possible . . . well, I finally did." She continued, "Are these worth anything?" The woman had a paper grocery bag filled with stock certificates. They were worth about $83,000. The certificates were dry now but had been soaked from water that had been sitting in her basement. And they smelled to high heaven. Had the woman not retrieved them when she did, they could have been completely lost in her basement and no one would have known how much they were worth.

Even if your financial affairs aren't that out of hand, there are good reasons to get a better handle on all the papers swirling around. Tax preparers charge less when they don't have to sort through a mess. And good records can substantially cut taxes you'll pay years from now when you withdraw money from an individual retirement account or sell a security or home. If people keep a good tally of home improvements, it could save them a fortune down the road. Perhaps even more importantly, organizing your files can make it easier for a spouse or other family member to pick up the pieces if you are suddenly not around. And it can be a valuable first step in getting a better handle on the assets you have and where your money goes. **Here is a list of some things to discard:**

* Most non-tax related checks more than one year old

* Expired insurance policies with no possible claim

* Records from cars and boats you no longer own

* All but the most recent cumulative pay stub for this year

* Clearly expired product warranties

Every home needs a system for the filing of personal records. No matter how modest your home facilities may be, you need a special place to keep tax records, legal items, insurance policies, and the like. The equipment you need does not have to be elaborate. A metal file cabinet is nice, but an accordion folder or a sturdy box with a lid will do just as well. The important thing is to keep everything together and organized—and to keep the system as simple as possible. It doesn't matter who organizes your home filing system, but utilize the talents of the person with the best organizational sense.

A simple subject file is all most people need for their everyday papers. Irreplaceable papers should be kept in a safe-deposit box, vault or safe. Do not keep your will in a safe-deposit box, however. If you choose to, make photocopies to keep in your home files. After you have completed your tax return, put all the receipts, W-2 forms, checks that relate directly to entries on that return, records of interest payments, medical expenses, real estate taxes, and whatever else may apply into a large manila envelope along with a copy of your tax return. This should prevent a bad case of nerves, should the IRS call you in for an audit. You only need to keep this packet for seven years but keep the tax returns themselves forever.

Remember to keep everything related to buying, selling, and improving a house (receipts, canceled checks, and contracts) indefinitely until you sell your last home. If you have deferred the profit tax (capital gains tax) by reinvesting your sales profit into another home, you will want to keep all of this information so that when you or your survivors finally make an accounting to the government, many of those expenses can be subtracted, decreasing the amount of taxable income.

Keep these in a safe-deposit box or home safe:

* Birth certificates
* Citizenship papers
* Marriage certificates
* Adoption papers
* Divorce decrees
* Stock and Bond certificates
* Passports

* Death certificates
* Titles to autos
* Deeds
* Household inventory
* Veteran's papers
* Insurance policies

You don't need canceled checks for posterity. Many financial planners say bank statements and routine checks for groceries and the like can be thrown out after a year. But make sure you keep canceled checks that substantiate tax deductions or verify major purchases. That is if you even get your checks back. Many banks no longer send them to you with your monthly statement. Not to worry, they are all on film at the bank and you can simply call them if you should need to verify anything for the IRS.

Always keep a written inventory of the items in every room of your home. This can be done quite efficiently with a home video camera. The value of each piece should be written somewhere to go along with the video.

Keep careful records of all contributions to nondeductible IRA's. When you pull money out of these retirement plans, the portion attributable to after-tax contributions won't be subject to tax. In any year you make a nondeductible IRA contribution, the Internal Revenue Service (IRS) says you should stow away copies of the form 8606 you file with your return, the first page of the tax return, and the annual statement you receive from the IRA trustee.

Insurance policies should all be kept somewhere safe. You can store these policies at home in a safe or in a safe-deposit box, but keep a list of all policies and agents. For your investments, have a separate folder for each mutual fund. Keep careful records of investments' costs to ease tax reporting and avoid over-paying tax when you sell. If your year-end mutual fund statements are cumulative (this means showing the full year's transactions) you can save just that one statement for each year. Keep all the confirmation notices for individual purchases. Make sure to note all stock splits. When you sell securities, file the purchase and sale records with a copy of your tax return.

Keep these items for "long-term" storage:

* Records of non-deductible IRA Contributions

* Death Certificates (even after the estate is settled)

* Military Records for possible veterans' benefits

* All tax returns and supporting documents for SIX years

* Information on possible pensions from former employers

PROFILE QUESTIONNAIRE— TAKE YOUR FINANCIAL INVENTORY 4

Before you can determine where you want your financial plan to take you, it's crucial to establish where you are right now. Take some time to assemble your financial records, and fill out the Profile Questionnaire worksheets at the end of this chapter. Where does all the money go? You'll have a pretty good idea once you have completed the Cash Flow and Personal Net Worth Worksheets.

It is my goal, by the end of this book, to have helped you to develop an accurate picture of your current financial status, assess your tolerance for risk, and determine how best to reach your long-term goals. I designed this questionnaire to help you anticipate the impact of milestone events on your financial goals and help you create a flexible financial plan.

Because financial planning depends upon an understanding of your current income needs as well as your long-term financial goals, it is important to determine who you are as an investor, what resources you have to invest, and where you want to go. Dealing with your future, in general, and financial planning, in particular, can sometimes seem a bit overwhelming.

I suggest you find a qualified financial advisor. The person you choose should have the knowledge and experience to evaluate your investment needs in light of your current financial situation, your long-term goals and the risk you are willing to assume. With all of these factors in mind, your advisor can suggest an investment strategy that will help you achieve your financial goals. The International

Association for Financial Planning (IAFP) offers free help in finding a planner. Call the IAFP at 1–800–945–4237. They will send you three things:

* A list of up to five financial advisors in your area

* A consumer Guide to Comprehensive Financial Planning, which contains basic planning information and tips on choosing a financial planner

* A financial advisor disclosure form you can use when interviewing planners to assess their qualifications and experience

We all have specific goals, but most of us share some basic financial needs. We may look to a secure retirement, owning a home, raising a family, and education for our children (or, in this day-in-age, our own continued education). For most of us, these are major, long-term goals that may take years to reach. On the other hand, short-term goals can include buying a new car, taking a vacation, or remodeling your home. It is my goal that this book will give you a starting point and help you focus on the future. Use it to develop your personal investment plan and to help you get your "financial house in order." By following these four time-honored strategies, you can create an investment plan that can help turn your dreams into reality.

1. *Invest for higher returns over the long term.* If you are an investor with long-term goals, you have an enormous advantage over people who are investing for the short term: TIME. The luxury of time allows you to look at long-term-oriented investments that are likely to offer the potential for higher rates of return.

2. *Diversify your portfolio.* By spreading your savings across a number of different investments you may achieve better long-term performance and consistency than investing in a single investment.

3. *Reduce risk.* While the average investor prefers to avoid excessive risk, being too conservative can cost greatly over the long term by causing you to miss opportunities.

4. *Consider mutual funds.* Managed by investment professionals, mutual funds can do the difficult work of investment research and diversification

for you, and since you can purchase or sell your mutual fund shares on any business day, you've got easy access to your money.

The secret to financial success is consistent growth. A solid plan will minimize both risk and the obstacles to success. Today, the average family spends more time planning their two-week vacation than their retirement, which can very well last as long as 25 to 30 years. Consequently, most women make financial decisions in a reactive manner (usually once their life relationship scenario has changed dramatically). Planning for the future is something most women have yet to make their top priority. Yes, I said your TOP priority. If you don't, all your financial moves will be in a reactionary mode. Keep in mind the only person who may be able to take care of the older citizen you will be someday is the younger person you are now. You must take personal responsibility for your finances, or at least be a contributing partner to your financial future with your significant other.

Making financial decisions in a reactive manner results in a depressing financial roller coaster ride of increasing and decreasing net worth. This roller coaster ride is inevitable when you fail to plan your finances. Understanding the roller coaster effect is instrumental in achieving financial success.

The dynamic nature of life directly affects our cash flow. You must see the "big picture" in order to avoid one of the most common reasons for financial failure—*saving to spend*.

Saving to spend is not necessarily a bad thing, but what we actually do is not always consistent with our goals. Accumulating wealth on a consistent basis is one of the most important methods to achieve financial success. Few people attain financial success from stock market speculation or winning the lottery.

This mental exercise may help you to better understand the power of systematic saving. Imagine for a moment that all of your assets (what you own) are gathered in a pile. Now imagine removing your liabilities (what you owe) from your assets. How big is the pile remaining? If you are like most women, what you have accumulated is wealth due to systematic saving. Examples of that are home equity, company pensions, 401(k) plans, 403(b) TSA's and life insurance cash values. I will discuss these types of investments in later chapters as well.

One of the most important, intangible assets is your risk management plan or insurance. I refer to insurance as an intangible because it is a key point that is often overlooked in wealth protection. Nonetheless, it is an extremely important part of your overall plan. Proper protection involves adequate property and casualty coverage, income replacement protection and "creditor-proofing" your assets. Inadequate protection of your assets can forever destroy your goal of financial success.

Despite efforts to the contrary, many women will still live in poverty during their retirement years. A recent study by the Department of Health and Human Services has highlighted the fact that few women achieve financial success prior to retirement. The study concluded for every 100 women starting their careers today, the following situation exists at age 65 . . .

29 have incomes under $7,000 (poverty level)

51 have annual incomes from all sources between $7,000 and $33,000, median income is $10,223

18 have died

2   have annual incomes over $33,000 (Yes, 2!)

I hope my point is coming across loud and clear. You *can* achieve financial success! However, planning your success is a necessity, not a luxury!

Let me give you six perspectives of financial planning which can help you focus on your financial goals. These concepts are based on the premise that your financial plan is only as strong as the weakest link. Consequently, considering the following may help you ensure yourself of a rock solid financial plan.

1.   If you live, your plan needs to be based on sound principles.

2.   If you become disabled or die, your plan needs to be solid.

3.   Your assets need to be protected from any litigation.

4.   Your plan needs to minimize the effects of taxes.

5.   Your plan needs to contain a provision for emergencies.

6.   Your plan needs to provide you with a secure retirement.

It is a paradox that in the world's richest nation, millions of women live in poverty.

These women did not plan to fail, they simply failed to plan. Don't allow yourself to fall into this trap of being financially unprepared.

HOW CAN WE ASSURE FINANCIAL SUCCESS?
BY TAKING THE FOUR STEPS THAT LEAD TO FINANCIAL INDEPENDENCE!

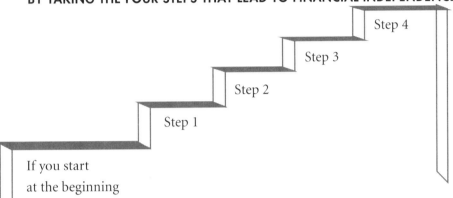

If you start
at the beginning
with no specific plan . . . then thoughout your working years you will not have saved enough and will only have spent what you earned . . . that leads to financial chaos at retirement.

If, however, you start from wherever you are now and develop a plan based on these four steps . . . you will have the financial independence you desire at retirement.

THE LONGER YOU WAIT . . .
THE STEEPER THE CLIMB

Step 1:   Set Financial Goals

Step 2:   Prioritize Those Goals

Step 3:   Initiate a "Plan of Action"

Step 4:   Review and Update the Plan Regularly

AN ESTATE PLANNING CHECKLIST

DO YOU HAVE THIS INFORMATION AND IS IT IN A SAFE PLACE?

Item	Location
Birth certificates	_____
Marriage certificates	_____
Wills and trust agreements	_____
Life, medical, disability and property insurance policies	_____
Social Security numbers	_____
Military discharge papers	_____
Stock and Bond certificates	_____
Real estate deeds	_____
Buy-sell (or other business agreements)	_____
Auto, boat or R.V titles	_____
Checking/savings account information	_____
Adoption papers	_____
Teacher's, nurse's or other work related license	_____
Diplomas (high school and/or college)	_____
Blueprints of home	_____
Abstract or title insurance for home	_____
Divorce decree or annulment papers	_____
Passports	_____
Six years of income tax returns	_____
Gift tax returns	_____

PROFILE QUESTIONNAIRE
YOUR SPENDING AND SPENDING HABITS

Most people spend first . . .
and try to save and invest
the little they have left

Few people set aside a definite
amount first . . . and only
spend the balance

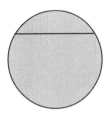

WHICH BEST DESCRIBES YOU?

If you're like the people in the first circle, you stand the chance of ending up with little or no savings or investment. If you're like the people in the second circle, however, you will find yourself accumulating dollars for education of children, retirement, and other worthwhile objectives. In other words, people in the second circle generally have money when they need it!

Personal Background

Your Name   Date of Birth   Social Security Number

Your Spouse   Date of Birth   Social Security Number

Address   City   State   ZIP

(____) _____   (____)_____
Home Phone   Work Phone

Your Occupation   Your Employer

Employer's Address   City   State   ZIP

Spouse's Occupation   Spouse's Employer

Employer's Address   City   State   ZIP

Is this account to be operated by anyone other than the owner?   ☐ yes   ☐ no
If yes please complete the information below

                                                          (____) _____
Name   Relationship to owner   Phone Number

Address   City   State   ZIP

Are you employed by or related to an employee of another brokerage firm?   ☐ yes   ☐ no

Are you an officer, director or owner of more than 10% of any public company?   ☐ yes   ☐ no

If yes, company name: _____

Family Information

(please list all children)

Should adopted children be treated as natural issue?	☐ yes	☐ no
Should adopted grandchildren be treated as natural issue?	☐ yes	☐ no
Should step children be treated as natural issue?	☐ yes	☐ no
Should step grandchildren be treated as natural issue?	☐ yes	☐ no

B = Children of current marriage   **A** = Adopted (specify C or S)
C = Client's child   **S** = Spouse's child
Please indicate one of the following for deceased children:
DC = Deceased with children   **DN** = Deceased, no children

Parent Codes (circle all applicable): B A C S DC DN

Child's full name _____ Date of Birth _____ Social Security Number

Address _____ City _____ State _____ ZIP

Smoker: ☐ yes ☐ no   List any known health problems: _____

Parent Codes (circle all applicable): B A C S DC DN

Child's full name _____ Date of Birth _____ Social Security Number

Address _____ City _____ State _____ ZIP

Smoker: ☐ yes ☐ no   List any known health problems: _____

Parent Codes (circle all applicable): B A C S DC DN

Child's full name _____ Date of Birth _____ Social Security Number

Address _____ City _____ State _____ ZIP

Smoker: ☐ yes ☐ no   List any known health problems: _____

Family Information (contd...)

Number of grandchildren: _____

Have you done any gifting of your assets to children or grandchildren?   ☐ yes   ☐ no

If so, how much to whom? _____

_____

Do you support anyone other than your children?   ☐ yes   ☐ no

If yes, who? _____

Business Interests

_____
Business Name

_____
Address   City   State   ZIP

(_____) _____   (_____) _____
Phone   Fax

_____
Type of ownership

If you were to sell your business interests today, what would be a fair market value? _____

Who will run this business upon death or disability of owner / shareholder? _____

Do you have a buy / sell agreement? ☐ yes   ☐ no
(If yes, obtain copy of agreement)

If so, how is it funded? _____

For what amount? _____

What type: ☐ Stock Redemption   ☐ Entity Purchase   ☐ Cross Purchase

Does it cover disability?   ☐ yes   ☐ no

Business Interests (contd...)

OWNERSHIP

Name	Position and/or Office	% Owned or Number of Shares	Total Value	Annual Direct	Other Compensation	Stock Options

Financial Background

What is your current tax bracket?
☐ 15%   ☐ 28%   ☐ 31%   ☐ 36% or higher

Over the next three years, do you expect your annual income to:

Increase_____%   Decrease_____%   Remain Constant

Rate your level of investment experience *(circle one)*

Novice 1 2 3 4 5 6 7 8 9 **Expert**

I am (we are) interested in...

Preparing an adequate college fund for our children or grandchildren	☐ yes	☐ no
Minimizing the taxes we pay on our income and investments	☐ yes	☐ no
Retiring comfortably at age _____	☐ yes	☐ no
Saving for a major purchase	☐ yes	☐ no
Making certain our family is financially secure in case of the untimely disability or death of the key financial provider(s)	☐ yes	☐ no
Receiving a higher return on my savings	☐ yes	☐ no
Budgeting and cash flow planning	☐ yes	☐ no
Establishing a systematic savings program	☐ yes	☐ no
Having income for the rest of my life	☐ yes	☐ no
Maximizing the inheritance our family will receive by minimizing state and federal estate taxes	☐ yes	☐ no
Building a contingency fund to cover financial emergencies	☐ yes	☐ no

Other: _____

_____

Financial Goals

We are currently using the following investment instruments to achieve our financial goals:

(please check all that apply)

- ☐ Bank savings account
- ☐ Life insurance
- ☐ Individual bonds
- ☐ Bond mutual fund
- ☐ Company 401(k) plan

- ☐ Certificate of deposit
- ☐ Disability insurance
- ☐ Individual stocks
- ☐ Equity mutual fund
- ☐ Company pension plan

- ☐ US savings bonds
- ☐ Variable annuity
- ☐ Money market fund
- ☐ Managed account
- ☐ Other_____

What else about your financial background would be helpful in determining your financial needs?_____

_____

_____

Please list other professionals with whom you currently work:

	Name	Address	Phone
Insurance Agent			
Attorney			
Investment Broker			
Accountant			

Investable Assets

(please list the dollar amount of your assets below)

Cash/Checking:*

Institution Name	Interest Rate	Dollar Amount

CDs*

Institution Name	Interest Rate	Dollar Amount	Maturity

Investable Assets (contd...)

Money Market Funds*

Name of Fund	Interest Rate	Dollar Amount
_____	_____%	$_____
_____	_____%	$_____

Life Insurance Cash Value*

Company	Interest Rate	Face Amount	Cash Value
_____	_____%	$_____	_____
_____	_____%	$_____	_____

Annuities*

Company	Interest Rate	Present Value	Type
_____	_____%	$_____	_____
_____	_____%	$_____	_____

Taxable and Tax-Exempt Bonds*

Type of Bond	Interest Rate	Current Value	Maturity
_____	_____%	$_____	_____
_____	_____%	$_____	_____
_____	_____%	$_____	_____

Stocks*

Number of Shares	Name of Company	Market Value
_____	_____	$_____
_____	_____	$_____
_____	_____	$_____

Mutual Funds*

Number of Shares	Name of Company	Market Value
_____	_____	$_____
_____	_____	$_____
_____	_____	$_____

Investable Assets (contd...)

Home*

	Market Value	Mortgage Payoff	Equity
	$ _____	– $ _____	= $ _____
	$ _____	– $ _____	= $ _____

Real Estate Investments (net after mortgage) and Limited Partnerships*

_____ $ _____

_____ $ _____

IRA / Keogh / 401(k) / SEP IRA / Other Pension*

Description	Year / Amount	Current Value	Maturity Date
_____	_____	$ _____	_____
_____	_____	$ _____	_____

TOTAL INVESTABLE ASSETS . . . . *$* _____
(retain figure for page 13)

Additional pages are provided in the back of this booklet

What portion of your gross annual income are you saving each year?

None_____   1–3%_____   4–7%_____   8–10%_____   10%+_____

Do you anticipate a major expenditure within the next five years?   ☐ yes   ☐ no

Net Worth Calculation

WHAT YOU OWN (ASSETS)

Investment Assets
(total from page 12) $ _____

Personal Property
Automobile(s) $ _____

Furniture/appliances $ _____

Jewelry $ _____

Collectibles and hobbies $ _____

Miscellaneous Assets
Loans people owe you $ _____

Business interests
(total from page 8) $ _____

Other $ _____

Total Assets $ _____

WHAT YOU OWE (LIABILITIES)

Current Bills
Auto loans $ _____

Installment loans $ _____

Taxes due $ _____

Credit card debit $ _____

Mortgages $ _____

Other debts $ _____

Total Liabilities $ _____

Calculate your net worth:

Total Assets $ _____

                                        minus

Total Liabilities $ _____

NET WORTH . . . . $ _____

Cash Flow Analysis

Monthly Expenses

Mortgage/Rent Payment	$ _____
Real Estate Taxes	$ _____
Home Maintenance/Supplies	$ _____
Electric	$ _____
Gas/Fuel	$ _____
Water/Sewer	$ _____
Refuse/Garbage	$ _____
Telephone	$ _____
Cable TV	$ _____
Home Equity/Improvement Loan	$ _____
Lawn/Pool/Snow Service	$ _____
Home Cleaning	$ _____
Other Loans	$ _____
Credit Cards	$ _____

Personal

Your Clothes	$ _____
Your Spouse's Clothes	$ _____
Child/Dependent Care	$ _____
Laundry/Dry Cleaning	$ _____
Personal Care/Hair Cuts etc.	$ _____
Groceries	$ _____
Restaurants	$ _____
Education	$ _____
Alimony/Child Support	$ _____
Vacations	$ _____
Entertainment/Recreation	$ _____
Children's Expenses/Allowances	$ _____
Books/Subscriptions	$ _____
Gifts/Cards	$ _____
Unreimbursed Business Expenses	$ _____
Charitable Contributions	$ _____

Automobiles

Auto Loan/Lease	$ _____
Replacement Fund	$ _____
Gas/Oil/License/Tolls/Parking	$ _____
Auto Insurance Premiums	$ _____
Repairs	$ _____

Personal Insurance Premiums

Disability Insurance	$ _____
Life Insurance	$ _____
Health Insurance	$ _____
Homeowners/Renters Insurance	$ _____

Unreimbursed Medical

Medicine/Prescription Drugs	$ _____
Physician Visits	$ _____
Nursing Care	$ _____
Dental Care	$ _____
Vision Care	$ _____

Home

Furnishings/Decor	$ _____
Appliances	$ _____

Miscellaneous	$ _____

TOTAL EXPENSES . . . . $ _____

Monthly Income

Wages, Tips Salary	$ _____
Spouse's Wages, Tips, Salary	$ _____
Bonuses, Commissions	$ _____
Interest & Dividends	$ _____
Alimony	$ _____
Child Support	$ _____
Capital Gains	$ _____
Social Security	$ _____
IRA Income	$ _____
Pensions	$ _____
Rent, Royalties, Partnerships	$ _____
Other Income	$ _____

TOTAL INCOME . . . . $ _____

Now subtract your total expenses from your total income to determine your cash flow for the month.

Risk Profile

The risk profile is divided into three sections: Time Horizon, Attitudes and Special Needs. There are no right or wrong answers. Simply circle the answer that is most representative.

TIME HORIZON

How many years remain until you will need the money to fund your most important financial goal?
1. 0 to 2 years
2. 2 to 5 years
3. 5 to 10 years
4. 10 years or more

ATTITUDES

Which of the three choices below do you feel best represents the type of investment you are seeking?
1. An investment that minimizes losses and account fluctuation in order to preserve principal
2. An investment that has some fluctuation accompanied by a higher expected return
3. An investment that strives for the highest possible return but that may have considerable fluctuation of account value

A $25,000 investment you made six months ago has dropped 10% in value. What would you do with this investment?
1. Sell immediately
2. Wait a few weeks to see if the investment turns around
3. Buy more of the investment. You believe this represents a good opportunity

How do you feel about investing in common stocks?
1. Common stocks should be used sparingly
2. Common stocks have a place in an investment portfolio
3. Common stocks are very attractive and should occupy a dominant position in a portfolio

What rate of return do you expect over a market cycle? (5-year period)
1. 6 – 8% average annual return
2. 9 – 11% average annual return
3. 12% or more average annual return

What "real" rate of return do you expect over inflation?
1. Maintain purchasing power
2. 1 – 2% above inflation
3. 3 – 4% above inflation
4. 5% or greater

Have you done any long-term care planning? ☐ yes   ☐ no

If so, what type (eg. home health care, nutrsing home insurance, adult day care insurance...)_____

_____

Risk Profile *(contd...)*

SPECIAL NEEDS

Do you have a need for income?　☐ yes　☐ no

If yes, state amount and frequency: _____

Based on your overall tax situation, is there a need for tax-exempt securities in your portfolio?　☐ yes　☐ no

Do you require a portion of your assets to be in cash at all times (excluding emergency fund)?　☐ yes　☐ no

If yes, please indicate size, either in market value or as a percentage of total portfolio assets: _____

Investing for College

If you want to start investing regularly for your child's education, the following steps will help you estimate the amount you will need to set aside. Table 1 and Table 2 on the back of this sheet will be used in making your calculations.

Step 1　Enter the number of years until your
　　　　child begins college　　　　　_____

Step 2　Enter the current **annual** cost of
　　　　the college your child will attend　$ _____

Step 3　Enter the appropriate inflation
　　　　factor from Table 1　　　　　_____

Step 4　Multiply the current annual cost by
　　　　the inflation factor. This equals your
　　　　child's future annual college costs　$ _____

Step 5　Multiply by 2 for a two-year college
　　　　or by 4 for a four-year college. This
　　　　equals your child's total estimated
　　　　college costs.　　　　　$ _____

Step 6　Select from Table 2 the investment
　　　　factor for the return you expect to
　　　　achieve after taxes　　　　　_____

Step 7　Multiply the total estimated cost (Step 5) by
　　　　the investment factor (Step 6). This is the
　　　　amount of money that you need to put aside
　　　　regularly each year to fund your child's educa-
　　　　tion. Divide this amount by 12 to obtain the
　　　　monthly figure, and divide by 52 for a weekly
　　　　figure.

　　　　Required Yearly Savings　　　$ _____

　　　　Monthly Savings　　　　　$ _____

　　　　Weekly Savings　　　　　$ _____

Investing for College (contd...)

TABLE 1

Years to
Start College — Inflation Factor

	4%	6%	8%	10%
1	1.04	1.06	1.08	1.10
2	1.08	1.12	1.17	1.21
3	1.12	1.19	1.26	1.33
4	1.17	1.26	1.36	1.47
5	1.22	1.34	1.47	1.61
6	1.27	1.42	1.59	1.77
7	1.32	1.50	1.17	1.95
8	1.37	1.59	1.85	2.14
9	1.42	1.69	2.00	2.36
10	1.48	1.79	2.16	2.59
11	1.54	1.90	2.33	2.85
12	1.60	2.01	2.52	3.14
13	1.67	2.13	2.72	3.45
14	1.73	2.26	2.94	3.80
15	1.80	2.40	3.17	4.18
16	1.87	2.54	3.43	4.59
17	1.95	2.69	3.70	5.05
18	2.03	2.85	4.00	5.56

TABLE 2

Years to
Start College — Investment Return, After Taxes

	4%	6%	8%
1	.981	.971	.962
2	.481	.471	.463
3	.314	.305	.296
4	.231	.222	.213
5	.181	.172	.164
6	.148	.139	.131
7	.124	.116	.108
8	.106	.098	.090
9	.093	.085	.077
10	.082	.074	.065
11	.073	.065	.058
12	.065	.058	.051
13	.059	.051	.045
14	.054	.046	.040
15	.049	.042	.035
16	.045	.038	.032
17	.041	.034	.029
18	.038	.031	.026

Retirement Profile

Desired annual retirement income:.................................... $ _____
Additional funds (to pay off a mortgage or other debt
  to make major post-retirement purchases):............................... $ _____

Expected annual retirement income:.................................... $ _____

Social Security: .... $ _____

Employer Pension Plan:.. $ _____

Pension Start Date: .... $ _____

Pension Indexed to Inflation:... $ _____

Part-Time Work Income:... $ _____

Retirement Profile (contd...)

How many years:.. _____

Amount you'll receive from asset & sales or other sources
(net profit from sales of other assets or amounts from gifts or inheritances):......... $_____

Current balance of tax-deferred retirement accounts
including employer plans, IRAs and individual plans): .... $_____

Amount you saved for retirement in taxable accounts:....................... $_____

Annual amount you're saving now:.................................... $_____

Annual amount your employer is contributing to your retirement account: .... $_____

Retirement Goals

			Rank
Adequate Retirement Income	☐ yes	☐ no	_____
Travel	☐ yes	☐ no	_____
Second Home	☐ yes	☐ no	_____
Recreational Vehicle	☐ yes	☐ no	_____
Continue to Work	☐ yes	☐ no	_____
Debt Free	☐ yes	☐ no	_____
Parental Care	☐ yes	☐ no	_____
Pass Assets to Heirs	☐ yes	☐ no	_____
Protect Against Nursing Home Costs	☐ yes	☐ no	_____

Other _____

_____

Insurance and Estate Planning

Do you have a will? ☐ yes ☐ no

If so, list the date of the will: _____

Have you established any trusts? ☐ yes ☐ no

If so, what type?
  ☐ Revocable living trust with marital trust and unified credit provisions
  ☐ Irrevocable life insurance trust
  ☐ Other

Pre-insurance concerns
Do you smoke? ☐ yes ☐ no
Do you have any known health problems? ☐ yes ☐ no

If yes, please list: _____

_____

Does your spouse smoke? ☐ yes ☐ no
Does your spouse have any known health problems? ☐ yes ☐ no

If yes, please list: _____

_____

Married clients
Date and place of marriage: _____

State of residence at date of marriage: _____

Did you sign a pre-nuptial (antenuptial) contract or agreement? ☐ yes ☐ no If so, attach a copy

During this marriage, if either of you have ever lived in a community property state (AZ, CA, ID, LA, NV, NM, TX, WA, WI), please specify the name of the state(s) and the date(s) of residence:

_____

Do you know of any person, such as a child from a previous relationship, previous spouse, or live-in partner who might make a claim against your estate? If so, please specify:

_____

Stocks and Bonds

Type and serial number	Ownership	Broker	Date Acquired	Original Value	Face Amount

Bank Accounts

Description	Bank/Branch Location	Account Number	Name Account Show In	Who Can Sign

Other Accounts

Description	Account Number	Name Shown Account Shown In

Notes Receivable

Name of Person/Business of Note Receivable	Amount and Terms

Real Estate

Description/Location	Purchase Price	Date Purchased	Value to Date

Miscellaneous Property

Description/Location	Purchase Price	Date Purchased	Current Value

Life Insurance

Type	Owner	Company/ Policy No.	Face Value	Due Date/ Amount	Primary Beneficiary	Secondary Beneficiary	Cash Value

Other Insurance

Type	Name of Company	Policy No.	Premium	Due Date

SOCIAL SECURITY AND WOMEN   **5**

Nearly every American—man, woman, and child—has Social Security protection, either as a worker or as a dependent of a worker. When the program began in 1935, Social Security benefits were limited to retired or deceased workers and their families, and most workers were men. Most women did not work outside the home at that time.

Today, the role of women is far different. Nearly 72 percent of all women are in the nation's work force. Many women work throughout their adult life. Although Social Security has always provided benefits for women, it has taken on added significance. More women work, pay Social Security taxes, and earn credit toward a monthly income for their retirement. Women with children earn Social Security protection for themselves and their families. This could mean monthly benefits to a woman and her family if she becomes disabled and can no longer work. If she dies, her survivors may be eligible for benefits.

Although some women choose a lifetime career outside the home, many women work for a few years, leave the labor force to raise their children, and then return to work. Some women choose not to work outside their home. They are usually covered by Social Security through their husband's work and can receive benefits when he retires, becomes disabled, or dies.

Whether you work, have worked, or have never worked, it is important that you know exactly what Social Security coverage means to you. You should also know about Social Security coverage for anyone you may hire as a household worker or provider of child care. You need to know what to do if you change your name. And you should know that if you receive a pension for work not covered by Social Security, your Social Security benefits could be affected.

When you work and pay Social Security taxes, you earn Social Security credits that can qualify you and your family for disability and survivors insurance coverage. You have this coverage whether you work for an employer or whether you are self-employed. You're also earning credits toward your retirement benefits. In addition, you're earning Medicare protection for yourself and your family in the event you, or they, ever need dialysis treatment or a kidney transplant. You're also earning Medicare protection that will be available when you reach age 65.

YOUR INVESTMENT IN SOCIAL SECURITY

You may wonder where your Social Security tax dollars go. Generally, out of every dollar you pay in Social Security taxes:

* 69 cents goes to a trust fund that pays monthly benefits to retirees and their families and to about 8 million widows, widowers, and children of workers who have died.

* 19 cents goes to a trust fund that pays for the health care of all Medicare beneficiaries

* 12 cents goes to a trust fund that pays benefits to people with disabilities and their families.

Your Social Security taxes also pay for administering Social Security. The administration costs are paid from the trust funds described above and are only about one cent of every Social Security tax dollar collected. Money not used to pay benefits and administrative expenses is invested in U.S. government bonds, generally considered the safest investments of all. The government uses money it has borrowed from Social Security (just as it uses money you may have invested in savings bonds) to pay for all the services and projects it provides for the U.S. citizens. Today, more than 45 million people, about one out of every six Americans, collect some kind of Social Security.

If you need a Social Security number, if you lost your card and need another one, or if you need to change your name on your current card, call or visit your local Social Security office or call the toll-free number 1–800–772–1213. You can get information 24 hours a day. You will be asked to complete a simple one-page form and show your birth certificate or a certified copy of it, and one other form of identification. If you are changing your name (due to marriage or divorce), you will need to show a marriage certificate or your divorce decree.

If you work for someone else, both you and your employer each pay 7.65 percent of your gross amount of pay for each pay period. This deduction is usually labeled "FICA" on your pay stub. This stands for the Federal Insurance Contributions Act, the law that authorized Social Security payroll tax. The Medicare tax is 1.45 percent which is paid by you and your employer (2.9% total).

If you are self-employed, you pay 15.3 percent of your taxable income into Social Security yourself and you are also responsible for the entire 2.9 percent of the Medicare tax.

You earn Social Security benefits by earning "CREDITS."

You must work and pay taxes into Social Security in order to get something back out of it (some people get benefits as a dependent or survivor on another person's Social Security record). As you work and pay taxes, you earn Social Security "credits." Currently you earn on credit for each $640 in earnings you have with a maximum of four credits per year. The amount of money needed to earn one credit goes up every year, so please check with the Social Security administration for the updated figure.

Most people need 40 credits (10 years of work) to qualify for benefits. Younger people need fewer credits to be eligible for disability benefits or for their family members to be eligible for survivors benefits if they should die.

If you become disabled and can't work for at least a year or your disability is expected to result in death, you can get disability benefits provided you have worked long enough under Social Security. Your disability payments would start with the sixth full month of your disability (there is a five month waiting period), and this would continue as long as you are disabled. If you receive disability payments for 24 consecutive months, you also have Medicare protection.

When you're disabled, your unmarried children can get benefits, too. Monthly checks are payable to your biological or legally adopted children, or dependent stepchildren or grandchildren who are under 18 years of age, become disabled before age 22 and remain disabled, or are age 18 to 19 and attending elementary or secondary school full time.

If you are married and your husband is age 62 or older, he may qualify for payments if you become disabled. He may qualify at any age if he is caring for your child, who is under age 16 or disabled and entitled to benefits.

When you die, both your widower and your dependent children may receive monthly survivors benefits. A one-time payment of $255 may be payable to your widower or dependent children.

SOME SPECIAL EMPLOYMENT SITUATIONS

If you and your husband own and operate a business together and you expect to share in the profits and losses, you may be entitled to receive Social Security credits as a partner. This may be true even if you and your husband have no formal partnership agreement. To receive credit for your share of the business income, you must file a separate self-employment return (Schedule SE), even though you and your husband file a joint income tax return. If you don't file a separate Schedule SE, all the earnings from the business will be reported under your husband's Social Security number. In that case, your Social Security record will not show your earnings, and you may not receive Social Security credits for them.

If you are a household worker, your wages are covered under Social Security if you earn $1,200 or more in 1997 (including cash for transportation expenses), unless you were under age 18 during any part of the year and household work is not your principal job. Household workers include babysitters, maids, cooks, laundry workers, butlers, gardeners, chauffeurs, people who do housecleaning or repair work, or anyone employed in or around someone else's home.

You should show your employer your Social Security card and ask him or her to withhold Social Security taxes from your wages, pay an equal amount, and send the combined taxes to the Internal Revenue Service with a report of the wages paid. If the wages aren't reported, you won't earn Social Security credit for your work. If you do not have enough Social Security credits, you and your family won't be able to get monthly benefits on your wage record when you retire, or if you become disabled or die. It's important that your earnings are reported even if you already have enough Social Security credits to entitle you to benefits. The amount of your benefit is based on your covered earnings over a period of years. If several years of earnings are omitted, your benefit may be lower than it would be if all your earnings are reported.

If you have served in the military on active duty or on inactive duty for training since 1957, you have paid into Social Security. Inactive duty service, in the Armed Forces Reserves and National Guard weekend drills, has been covered by Social Security since 1988. If you served in the military before 1957, you did not pay into Social Security directly, but your records may be credited with special earnings for Social Security purposes that count toward any benefits you may be entitled to receive.

When you apply for Social Security, the credits you receive for military service are added to your civilian work credits. The number of credits you have determines whether you qualify. You may be eligible for both Social Security benefits and military retirement. Generally, there is no offset of Social Security benefits because of your military retirement. You will get your full Social Security benefit based on your earnings. Your Social Security benefit may be reduced, however, if you receive a pension from a job in which you did pay Social Security taxes.

WHEN YOU RETIRE

You may be able to get Social Security benefits as early as age 62, but your benefit will be permanently reduced to account for the longer time that you will receive checks. If you wait until 65 to retire, you'll be eligible for full retirement benefits (starting in 2003, the age at which full benefits are payable will be increased gradually until it reached 66 in 2009 and 67 in 2027).

If you are married, you can receive retirement payments on you own record or spouse's benefits on your husband. Your husband can get retirement benefits at age 62 or older, either on his record or as a spouse on your record. People who are eligible for benefits on more than one work record generally receive the larger benefit amount.

If you've had high earnings, it is likely that your own benefits will be higher than a spouse's. On the other hand, if you stopped working for several years or had lower earnings, the spouse's benefit may be higher. At 65, a wife receives 50 percent of what her husband is entitled to at 65.

IF YOU'VE NEVER BEEN EMPLOYED

If you make your home and family your career, you and your family have Social Security protection through your husband's work. You can receive benefits when he retires, becomes disabled, or dies.

You can receive payments if you are caring for a child who is under 16 or disabled entitled to benefits. If you don't have a child in your care, you must be 62 years old or older to get benefits when your husband becomes disabled or retires.

If you choose to begin receiving retirement benefits before age 65, your benefits amount will be permanently reduced. If you wait until you are age 65, you'll get the full wife's benefit, which is the 50 percent mentioned earlier.

You will be entitled to Medicare hospital insurance at age 65 if your husband is entitled to monthly benefits. You will have Medicare at age 65 even if your husband is younger than you and still working, provided he is at least 62 and will be entitled to benefits when he retires. You should file an application for Medicare (hospital insurance) at least three months before you reach age 65.

WHEN YOUR MARITAL STATUS CHANGES

If your husband dies, you can receive widow's benefits if you are age 60 or older. If you are disabled, you can get widow's benefits as early as age 50. The amount of your monthly payment will depend on your age when you start getting benefits. It also will depend on the amount your deceased husband would have been entitled to, or was receiving, when de died.

Widow's benefits range from $70\frac{1}{2}$ percent of the deceased husband's benefit amount if they begin at age 60, to 100 percent if they begin at age 65. So, if you start receiving benefits at age 65, you'll get 100 percent of the amount your husband would be receiving if he were still alive (starting in 2005, the age at which the 100 percent widow's benefit is payable will be increased gradually until it reaches 66 in 2011 and 67 in 2029).

If you are a disabled widow between the ages of 50 and 59, your monthly benefit would be 70 $\frac{1}{2}$ percent of your deceased husband's benefit amount.

Here are some important points to remember:

1. If you are entitled to retirement benefits on your own work record, you can take reduced retirement payments at age 62 and then receive the full widow's benefit at age 65.

2. You can receive a widow's benefit at age 60 and get your full retirement benefit at age 65.

3. If you remarry, you will continue to receive benefits on the deceased husband's or deceased ex-husband's Social Security record. However, if you current husband is a Social Security beneficiary, you may want to apply for a wife's benefit on his record if it would be larger than you widow's benefit. YOU CANNOT DO BOTH!

IF YOU GET DIVORCED

You can receive benefits on your ex-husband's Social Security record if he is receiving Social Security benefits (or is deceased) and these criteria are met:

* Your marriage lasted 10 years or longer

* You are presently unmarried

* You are age 62 or older

If your ex-husband has not applied for benefits, but can qualify for them and is age 62 or older, you can receive benefits on his record if you have been divorced from him for at least two years and meet the requirements listed above. If your ex-husband is deceased, you can receive benefits on his record even though you were not married to him for 10 years if you are caring for his child who also is your natural or legally adopted child, who is under the age of 16 or disabled, and you are currently unmarried. Your benefits will continue until the child reaches age 16 or the child's disability ceases. The amount of benefits you receive as a divorced spouse does not affect the amount of benefits another spouse receives on your ex-husband's record.

Many women get a higher benefit based on their ex-husband's work record than they would get on their own record, especially if he is deceased. If you've never asked Social Security about receiving benefits on your ex-husband's record, you should do so **now**. When you apply, you will need his Social Security number. If you don't know his number, you'll need to provide his date and place of birth and his parent's names.

IMPORTANT NOTE: THE SAME CONDITIONS APPLY TO A DIVORCED HUSBAND WHOSE ELIGIBILITY FOR BENEFITS IS BASED ON HIS EX-WIFE'S SOCIAL SECURITY RECORD.

It's a good idea to request an accounting from the Social Security Administration regularly throughout your working years to find out if your Social Security records are correct. Simply call the Social Security Administration at 1–800–772–1213 and ask for a "*Request for Earnings and Benefits Estimate Statement.*" Return the form, and within a month you'll get a personalized statement detailing the amounts you've paid into the system. The statements also provide estimates of your Social Security payments if you retire when you're 62, 65 or 70. Since mistakes can occur, and it becomes more and more difficult to correct them with the passing years, the Social Security Administration recommends that you check your records about every three years. Social Security treats all calls confidentially whether they are made to the toll-free number or to your local office.

WHAT RELATIONSHIP/ LIFE SCENARIO ARE YOU IN?

6

Choosing an investment approach begins with understanding your individual needs and your current "relationship scenario." Now that you know what you are worth, take a look at some of the typical investor relationship scenarios. While these are broad categories and do not apply to everyone, chances are you will find some themes similar to your own situation.

SINGLE: JUST GETTING STARTED

"The important thing is to start now."

When you are young and just starting out, you need to build for the future. That's often the greatest hurdle. But once you begin, you'll feel more confident and in control of your money—and your future. More than likely, you earn just enough to cover your current expenses, with little left over for savings. At this stage, your investment objectives should involve major, long-term lifestyle goals. You don't need extensive financial knowledge, or a high income, a large sum of money, or a great deal of time. You do need to make investing a priority. Your goals should include:

* Paying off school loans

* Finding a post-graduate job that pays well

* Saving for a major purpose such as a new car

* Budgeting for independent living costs such as housing, food, etc.

* Beginning a sound retirement program (yes, even if you've just landed your first job, retirement planning is essential).

It can take less money than you think to get started. Starting now benefits you because the longer you invest, the more opportunity your money has to grow. You'll be amazed at how small, regular investments can really add up. By saving small amounts on a regular basis, you can make an appreciable investment over time. And remember, the sooner you begin, the easier it will be to seek your goals and to help provide the income you'll need many years from now when you retire. Just because it seems like an eternity from now—don't put it off!

Here are five easy steps to getting started:

1. Make it a priority: It won't happen unless you make a concerted effort to begin. So start organizing your financial life by putting it at the top of your list.

2. Get going: The most important thing is to *act*. No one can do it but you, and the sooner you start, the easier it will be to reach your financial goals. You don't need to worry if you're new to investing—what you do need to do is be willing to learn.

3. Seek help: While you're responsible for your financial well-being, you don't have to determine your investment strategy alone. A financial advisor can help you create an investment program to meet your needs. Try asking friends and relatives for the names of financial advisors they recommend.

4. Listen, read, learn, and ask: You'll be making decisions with your financial advisor, so try to understand the basics but don't be afraid to ask questions.

5. Don't worry: Investing is a lot easier than you think. It's no more complicated than the issues you face each day at home or work. While investing does involve risks, the main thing you really need to worry about is *not* acting.

MARRIAGE: COMBINING TWO FINANCIAL LIVES

Just as communication and compromise help make romantic dreams come true, they also make it easier to realize financial dreams and goals. Openness is essential when two people merge their personal and financial lives. This is easier said than done, since in many cases one or both parties marrying today have been financially independent for some time, and are not accustomed to sharing details about their financial situation. Although traditionally marriage has been thought of as something for the younger group, please take into account that this can occur during any stage of an adult's life. For some people this can be occurring for a second or even third time.

No matter what your financial situation, you must work together to create a monthly budget that lists income and expenses. Some budget problems that couples experience are due to lack of information. Both partners may have access to checkbooks and credit cards, but are unaware of how much each of them spent until the end of the month. Decide now how you will share both expenses and paperwork, and then stick with the plan. Keep in mind that while combining finances may give you more economic clout, it's important that each partner keep some accounts in his or her own name to maintain individual credit history.

Couples who make an effort to focus on what they really want often find that the process helps give direction and propels them toward realizing their goals. There's no mystery to achieving financial goals provided you take one important step: saving a portion of your income on a systematic basis. Try to "pay yourself first" by setting aside part of your current income before you pay the monthly bills. It's never too early—or too late—to start putting aside money for any goals you may have.

Goals at this lifestyle stage could include:

* Buying a home
* Finance handling (shared responsibility)
* Successful pooling of financial resources
* Proper distribution of financial resources
* Increasing current income

* Financing recreational activities or longer vacations

* Purchasing major items

* Concentrating more on retirement savings

When you're in mid-career you may need more income and nest-egg protection. Mid-career investing stage objectives often involve maintaining the quality of your current lifestyle with increased income, while building a larger base of assets.

UPDATING YOUR RECORDS DUE TO MARRIAGE

Even as you plan your wedding and your budget, there are a number of details that should be taken care of. First, make a list of records that will require name changes. These could include the beneficiaries on life insurance policies, pension plans and profit-sharing plans. It's also important to notify the Social Security Administration of your marriage so you'll become eligible for your spouse's benefits. If a woman changes her name, she should make the change on her driver's license, credit cards, employment records and other forms of identification. Secondly, prepare a list of items that may have financial implications for your new household. If you both work, check to see whether or not overlapping benefits mean that you and your spouse will be overinsured. At the same time, adjust your auto insurance policy to take advantage of favorable rates due to your new marital status. Also review your property insurance to make sure you have enough coverage for your combined possessions. In terms of taxes, you'll likely need to adjust your W-4 and state withholding form to make allowances for the proper deductions.

Finally, while you're rearranging your financial affairs, each of you should write or rewrite your will. You and your new significant other should also use the "Financial Goals" worksheet. You may just find that it is a springboard for discussion as you anticipate your major expenses for the coming years. Try to be as specific as possible as you investigate the various alternatives for using your financial resources. You should also take the time to regularly review and update the worksheet and recalculate the amount you'll need to reach your goals.

DIANE K. KEISTER

PROVIDING FOR CHILDREN:

The birth of a child is a turning point for any family, and you'll want to provide your child with every possible advantage. One of the best ways to fulfill your expectations is to have a sound financial plan right from the start.

According to government estimates, it may take approximately $275,000 over 21 years to raise a child born in 1997. And that will cover only the necessities: food, clothing, housing, transportation and medical bills (those not covered by insurance). Education expenses will substantially increase the cost. By taking the time to outline future plans, evaluate options and make hard financial decisions in advance, you'll be better prepared for the expenses you and your family will face over the years.

What do you want for your child?

All families have different views about what is essential for a child's development. This may include athletic training, piano lessons, summer camp, or personal computers.

What do you think your child will require to become a happy and successful adult?

It is wise to begin setting aside money as early as possible for the advantages you want to provide. For dual-income families, advanced financial planning is of special concern, since the birth of a child may mean reduced income and diminished savings power. Even families in which both parents continue to work will find it harder to save once a child is born, since child care and preschool expenses will command a large part of their budget.

No matter what your child's future holds, the most expensive advantage you can provide is a college education. In the 1996–97 school year, the average cost for four years at a public college was $28,540, and $64,320 for years at a private institution. Most experts believe that increases in college costs will continue to out pace inflation. At that rate, four years at a public college could reach $68,300 by 2005, and over $194,000 at a private college.

The key to successfully saving enough money for college is to begin early. The sooner you develop a systematic savings plan, the more time you'll have to accumulate the funds you need. Ideally, you should begin saving for college even before your child or grandchild is born. But even if the child is already in school, it's not too late to start.

You should take special care to protect your children in the event of an emergency. If you're anticipating the birth of a child, take steps to purchase life insurance and formulate an estate plan. You may also want to consider the benefits of setting up a trust for the child:

1. Purchase life insurance or review the benefits of your existing policy, and consider naming your child as a contingent beneficiary.

2. Review your health insurance policy. If you and your spouse are covered by individual plans, consider a family plan with the broadest benefits. A change in coverage, however, many times needs to take place prior to you becoming pregnant. Sometimes the insurer will also have a 30, 60 or even 90 day clause. This means that you would have needed to change insurance coverage at least that much time in advance of notifying them that you have become pregnant. And remember also, to be eligible for coverage, most health insurers require notification within 30 days of the child's birth.

3. Develop or update your will and name a guardian for your child. I think you should strongly consider each parent having an individual will with durable power of attorney and health care power of attorney, naming the other parent to act as agent if that become necessary. You could, however, designate anyone, preferably over age 21, to act as your agent. This should be someone that you trust with your life.

4. Consult an attorney regarding the advantages of setting up a trust for your child or perhaps even a Revocable Living Trust for yourself, depending on your financial situation.

A NOTE ABOUT THE TRANSFERS TO MINORS ACT:

Beginning in 1955 under the sponsorship of the Association of Stock Exchange Firms, the model "Act concerning Gifts of Securities to Minors" proposed by the New York Stock Exchange was enacted in 14 states and the District of Columbia. This law had as its objective the cutting of legal red tape to make it possible for the outright gift of securities to a minor, while at the same time reserving the power of management to a custodian until the minor attained 21 years of age.

The model Law was succeeded in 1956 by a shorter, improved statute called the "Uniform Gift to Minors Act." Upon the recommendation of the Association of Stock Exchange Firms and the New York Stock Exchange, the National Conference of Commissioners of Uniform Laws (the "Conference") adopted the UGMA and recommended its enactment in every state and territory. Revisions of UGMA were effected by the Conference in 1965 and 1966.

All states and territories adopted the UGMA in some form. However, over the years various states enacted non-uniform amendments for specific purposes. For instance, some jurisdictions have felt the need to expand the kinds of property that could be given, while other states amended the Act to permit transfers from trusts and estates. As a result, the Conference felt that an important aim of the original Act—uniformity—had been lost. This created potential conflicts of law in situations where the law of more than one jurisdiction may have applied to a transaction or series of transactions

In 1984 the UGMA was replaced with a new model statute. Since the UGMA's limitation on the property that may be transferred to a custodian and its limitation to lifetime gifts by a donor have both been superseded, the name of the new statute was changed to the "Uniform Transfers to Minors Act" ("transfers" being a broader term than "gift"). The adoption of this Act in place of the UGMA was recommended to various states and territories by the Conference, and many states have since adopted the UTMA. The only states which are still under the UGMA laws now, in 1998, are Michigan, South Carolina, Vermont and the Virgin Islands.

The importance of the transaction should not be minimized. One overriding factor must be kept in mind in considering making a transfer under the statute:

A transfer under these laws is a complete, irrevocable transfer of one's interest to the minor. The transferor gives up all rights to the property, and the transfer may not be revoked under any circumstances there is simply no way that the property transferred under these laws can be returned to the transferor. Accordingly, the transferor must be certain of his or her decision prior to making the transfer.

Transfers under the UGMA or the UTMA are irrevocable, so that unforeseen tax consequences cannot be corrected after the fact. As a result, prudence suggests that someone contemplating a transfer should consult with a tax advisor prior to the transaction, particularly if the transfer or a group of transfers exceed $10,000.

YOUR MID-LIFE YEARS

The years that separate young adults from senior citizens can be exciting and demanding. Faced with career and family responsibilities, many of us feel too busy to plan ahead for our retirement. However, it's critical that by the time you reach your 40s and 50s, you've calculated how much money you'll need for a comfortable retirement. There are ways for you to make the most of your savings, so you can start to establish a retirement plan that meets your needs. In the chapter on retirement, I've provided additional worksheets to assist you in your endeavor to make a secure retirement.

Your peak earning years will probably coincide with your peak spending ones—during your 40s and 50s. But as you get closer to retirement, your focus should shift from earning and accumulating assets to the equally daunting task of making them available throughout your retirement years. Since the average life expectancy of a woman who has reached age 65 is now 85 years old, many will need a retirement income for 20 years or more. In my estimation, any woman today should plan for a full 30 years in retirement. With medical advances being what they are and new ones being developed every day, it would be devastating to have additional years and no money to support yourself. Not only must you plan for the first year of retirement, but you also have to consider your last.

By the time you reach the mid-life stage, you should have an idea of how social security and pension benefits will contribute to your retirement. The charts in the chapter on retirement help you to estimate annual social security payments, but keep in mind that the current payment schedule could change more than once as you become eligible to collect. Among full-time workers in 1996, 42% of women weren't covered by pension plans at all.

In addition to planning for a secure retirement, a variety of expected and unexpected events could increase your financial pressures during mid-life. For example, many parents will be facing enormous education costs for their children. Also, post-teen and college-educated children may remain or return home until they feel financially independent. Financial pressure could come from grown children with families as well. With the high divorce rate, many single parents are forced to turn to their own parents to provide financial support. And finally, you could be called upon to provide emotional and financial help to elderly parents in poor health. While these situations are not likely to affect all of us, it would be helpful to build a special nest egg so you can be in a position to help out if the need arises.

While your own circumstances will determine the amount that's right for you, generally, I would recommend that people more than 20 years from retirement should go for growth, and allocate 70% or more of their assets to stocks or stock funds. If you are 10 years or less from retirement, this figure, in my estimation, should only go down to 60% of your investment portfolio in equities. It's important to keep in mind the amount of money you'll need to save for retirement and the risk you're willing to assume to achieve your goal. If your strategy is too conservative, you may lock yourself into a return that's too low to meet your goals because of inflation's adverse effects.

STRATEGIES FOR RETIREMENT YEARS

There used to be a simple rule in financial planning for retirement: Safety first! Shortly before embarking on their round-the-world cruises, retirees often converted their assets into conservative income-producing investments. But times have changed! Since the average U.S. life expectancy (for men and women combined) is nearly 80 years, one of a retiree's main objectives should be keeping up with inflation. Increased health care costs in particular could cause problems for this group. I'd like to stress the importance of keeping your financial plan flexible, and your investment portfolio well diversified.

A key element of any plan is taking the time to periodically review your finances. The "Profile Questionnaire" is not designed to be used only once. If you have done a similar type of exercise in the past, please take the time to complete this one as well. Also, I do feel this questionnaire is more complete than many others you will find. By updating the "Profile Questionnaire" regularly throughout the different stages of your life, you can adjust your portfolios assets as needed.

Although current income is the main concern of most retirees, the probability of an extended retirement period often makes it essential for the newly retired to continue to invest for a greater return than fixed income investments typically provide. To stay ahead, a sound strategy would include increasing wealth by looking beyond yield and by investing in securities with appreciation potential in addition to those producing current income. The charts here show one suggestion as to how to diversify your portfolio during early retirement vs. later in retirement.

As you can see, placing assets in a variety of securities, including stock and bond mutual funds, money market accounts and balances mutual funds can reduce your risk because your portfolio will be diversified. For investors with a more aggressive approach, this may include many more individual stock companies. While, for those with a more conservative approach, this may mean only corporate and other individual bonds. Based, of course, on your individual situation, you may even put a small portion of your assets into such things as commodities or futures. These are investment that hedge against inflation. Other investments may include gold (in the form of funds or coins), and even real estate. This could be rental property, REITs, which are Real Estate Investment Trusts, or Real Estate Partnerships. For the purposes of this book, I have kept the discussions to mostly the basics. Some forms of investment "strategies" are discussed in another chapter. For the most part, I've tried to make this first edition as simple as possible. The point I'm trying to make here is that, ultimately, allocation of your portfolio depends on your personal circumstances, and as you work with a financial advisor you will be able to develop as investment strategy that is right for you!

SUDDENLY SINGLE: FINANCIAL LIFE AFTER THE DEATH OF A SPOUSE

The death of a spouse is an immense emotional loss, but it also involves a number of urgent financial and legal matters. Despite their grief, surviving partners must face important decisions as they begin to look towards the future. In this section, I'll be focusing on topics that should be addressed as soon as possible after the death of your spouse. Although it may be unpleasant to address these issues today, advance planning could make them easier to face tomorrow.

Perhaps the best advice one can give to those who've lost their loved one is to avoid making major changes or life-changing decisions in the early stages of grief. Of course, there are many necessary details like paying bills and claiming death benefits that must be dealt with immediately. But I suggest that financial decisions, including whether to sell a home or how to manage assets, should be postponed for six months to a year if circumstances allow. In order to make realistic plans for the future, it's essential to know how much money is available to spend and what you must spend it on. This is where the "Profile Questionnaire" should make it easy to record your income and expenses in order to establish a budget that includes a savings or investment plan. This is why I had stated earlier that you will need to update your information. It is very important to have it reviewed with your significant other at least once every year so that you know exactly what has been happening. Even if, at this point, your spouse handles all of the household financial paperwork, make it your task to complete and update the questionnaire at least annually.

While you may already have a budget, your spouse's death could trigger changes in your financial situation significant enough to require a new one. Jane Bryant Quinn, the popular author of the book *Making the Most of Your Money*, prefers to call budgets spending plans, since they allow you to take control of your finances. "A spending plan," she says, "starts from where you are now and makes things better." So don't make the mistake of thinking that "budgeting" implies a financial shortfall that requires cutting expenses. Your personal budget should really be a plan that leaves plenty of room for choice. Your budget shows how much you have to live on, as well as whether or not you have extra savings to invest.

Income and estate taxes could have a serious impact on a surviving spouse's total financial picture. For example, if the person who died owned property in two states, the estate may owe taxes in both. You'll need a thorough understanding of your tax liabilities in order to have a realistic picture of your long-range net worth and short-term cash flow. It may be wise to seek the advice of an accountant on these matters, ask your financial advisor or friends to recommend someone.

If you have no dependents, you may choose to drop your life insurance altogether. However, if you have dependents and are still working, you should consider increasing life insurance and adding disability insurance. Make sure you change any beneficiary designations that name your spouse, if you continue to be insured. Group coverage should continue if your health insurance was covered by your spouse's policy, and you may be able to convert to an individual policy when that coverage ends.

If you are 65 or older, a Medigap policy for medical expenses not covered by Medicare could provide an extra measure of security. Your net worth may increase after the death of your spouse, but whether you've inherited money or not, you should revise your own estate plan. That would include having your will rewritten, and at the same time, taking steps to retitle your jointly held assets and record changes in beneficiary designations for savings and investment programs.

Many women find it helpful to spend time clarifying investment goals after the death of their spouse. In particular, widows who receive large financial settlements may seek the services of a qualified financial advisor for help in assessing your needs. If you haven't worked with a financial advisor before, be sure that you understand in advance any cost of developing your financial plan, and the fees and/or commissions for investment transactions. These are different from advisor to advisor.

Especially after the death of your spouse, you should avoid taking financial actions that you don't understand or that make your feel uncomfortable. Please also be sure you understand the reasons for any recommendations, and how they fit into your personal financial plan.

A FINANCIAL CHECKLIST: 8 THINGS TO TAKE CARE OF RIGHT AWAY

1. Notify your spouse's employer immediately. Later, discuss any final or deferred compensation you may be entitled to, as well as life insurance, pension and profit-sharing benefits, and, if appropriate, accident insurance with the employee benefits office. Ideally, all these things should be known by you *now* so that you are familiar with your benefits when the time comes.

2. Contact your funeral director. Make necessary arrangements. This, too, should be arranged as mush as possible ahead of time (Unfortunately, many men do not see the need to have this subject discussed or arranged prior to anything happening to them). It may be helpful for you to call and ask some questions ahead of time, however.

Ask the funeral director for 10 to 15 certified copies of the death certificate, so you'll be able to file insurance claims and Social Security claims and retitle joint accounts.

3. Ask your lawyer about the proper way to retrieve the contents of a safe-deposit-box. In some states, it may take a court order. Once you've located your spouse's will, request that your lawyer take steps to begin the probate process. Again, you may want to contact a lawyer now to ask about a Revocable Living Trust. This type of trust usually avoids probate.

4. Notify your insurance agent to file a claim, and Social Security to file for benefits. If your spouse was a veteran, notify the Veterans Administration also.

5. Locate all accounts (be sure to check with all investment brokers in your area), and have them converted to your name only. This should include your vehicle registration(s).

6. It may prove helpful to write to any union, professional or fraternal organization(s), alumni association, and other groups your spouse may have belonged to. Membership might entitle you to death benefits (usually through group life insurance).

7. Accumulate the paperwork for outstanding debt and promissory notes. Check with local lenders too see if any debt (loans) carried an insurance rider that would pay the debt in full at death. I can't stress this enough, please try to know this information ahead of time. This will be a very emotional period in your life and you should not have the extra burden of trying to find out all of these facts.

8. Cancel all extra credit cards or convert them to your name only.

You may wish to send letters to the various organizations I've mentioned above. The technical terms some investment professional use every day may be foreign to you. Here are a few helpful "jargon" terms explained:

Technical Term	Explanation
Basis Point	Percentage Point
Capital Appreciation	Growth
Compounding	Automatic reinvestment of interest, dividends, and any gains
Dollar Cost averaging	Systematic investing
Equities	Stocks
Debt (Fixed Income Securities)	Bonds
Load	Charge
Liquidity	East access to your money
Maturity	Date the investment comes due
Principal	Your original investment

IS MONEY THE GREAT EQUALIZER?

You'd think so. It's a straight forward, unambiguous measure for men and women alike. If you're good at making, keeping, and spending money, it shouldn't matter whether you're male or female.

But it does matter!

I was having coffee with a group of friends and one woman, who is married, said, "I don't have anything to do with our money. I don't know where it is or where it goes." Her paycheck goes into a joint account; she does fund a pension, but when I asked if she chose how the pension was invested, she said, "No, my husband took care of that for me."

I'm surprised by how inactive many women are in their own money management and how ill-prepared they are for the many lifestyle changes that can blindside a woman at any given moment. Women often take control of their finances in the wake of a crisis: divorce, illness, unemployment, or death of their spouse. Confronting financial realities during periods of emotional stress is not good. To avoid this, it's essential to be prepared.

Part of the problem is how investment advisors, in general, have treated women. It sounds as if women are intimidated because they don't understand the language of finance. They're embarrassed. That's why I think sometimes women do better with female investment advisors.

This comes from, in large part, our social conditioning. I had a fourth grade teacher who said to me, "You're not very good at math but don't worry about it, you won't need it, your husband will deal with those things." Many aspects in our education system have changed since I was in the fourth grade. Let's hope that's one of them.

Today, women investors are different because they're getting money differently. It's a different round of education. One statistic I came across indicated that women switch jobs every 4–5 years. With only this number of years at a job, women leave before they actually get vested in pension plans. This leaves them having to shoulder much more of the burden of retirement financing.

In a survey completed by Smith Barney of their client base, they found that 61 percent of males characterized themselves as aggressive as opposed to only 14 percent of women. The reality of it, though, is that women are much better at making a plan. They will stay the course toward their goal. Guys treat investments like sports. They're out there shooting, but not hitting very much. They'll tend to buy into and sell out of mutual funds quite readily. They won't be quite as goal-oriented. Women aren't watching what the S&P is doing every hour, but men are glued, watching CNBC, figuring out how they're going to outsmart the next market fluctuation (like outsmarting their opponent on the other side of the net). That's aggressive, I guess. It's certainly different. So, being a woman can be a tremendous asset in the world of investments!

HERE'S WHAT OTHER WOMEN HAVE EXPRESSED:

Can you see yourself in any of these situations?

Barbara—

"Frankly, I was frustrated about my financial situation. I needed help. I'm self-employed, and in my work there can be "dry" spells. I really love what I do, but the problem is, the bills are always coming in ... even when the money isn't. I'd always have this blind spot when it came to money. I'd grown up believing a knight in shining armor would sweep me off my feet and take all my financial worries away." This woman continued, "Well, I'd learned to rely on myself, but I was reluctant to ask for help when it came to managing money. After being independent for so long, I was afraid a financial advisor would talk down to me or take advantage of the fact I didn't know much about investing. Looking back, it's strange that I was so willing to hand over financial control to a husband, but was hesitant to talk to an investment professional who could help me gain control. I have one now and I'm very happy with her."

Susan—

"I assumed we were saving enough . . . we were doing fairly well. So I was devastated when our accountant said we may fall short at retirement—that was only 4 years away. We hadn't enough time to make up that amount. My husband used to make our investment decisions and pay the bills so, to me, hearing the Dow Jones report was like hearing sports scores. What's funny is that I worked part-time as a bookkeeper so I was very comfortable with numbers. Even so, I thought the financial markets were different. Well, after I got the news, that's when I began to get involved. Now my husband and I make all of our decisions together. We are still pinching pennies, but I think about what could have happened if I hadn't opened my eyes at all."

Kathy—

"Risk was not what I was looking for when I started investing. My husband had always handled the money—he was a tax attorney after all. I never had to give it much thought. But, after the divorce, I found myself in an unfamiliar world of paying bills, keeping a budget, and even selling a house. I was so afraid of losing money that I put it all in a savings account. It felt safe. I just wanted everything to settle down. I needed that kind of security. But after a while, I realized it wasn't earning much, the money wasn't growing enough, and I began to worry about retirement. It took this new fear to get me over my old fear of losing money. That was what motivated me to take the next step. I did some homework, talked to friends, then found someone who could help me. After reading a lot of magazines and discussing the topic with my new advisor, I invested in mutual funds. It was important to have access to my money if I needed it. I'm really proud of my daughters. They've started investing on their own. It makes me feel good knowing they'll be prepared.

Women who shy away from investing are asking for trouble. Investing is not an option for women. It's a necessity. There are four basic investment errors that most women make. They are:

1. Investing too little

2. Investing too conservatively

3. Beginning an investment strategy too late

4. Doubting your ability to manage your hard-earned money.

Responsible investing begins with education and understanding. Market corrections eventually happen, and staying focused on long-term goals can potentially help through unpredictable times.

USING CREDIT WISELY

7

Thinking single when it comes to credit isn't disloyal or unromantic, it's smart. It's the way to build a record of your own and avoid problems if something happens to your spouse, or your marriage ends in divorce. But credit, especially credit cards, can be a double-edged sword. Learn to manage it so it works to your benefit, not to undercut your financial plan.

BUILD A CREDIT "HER"STORY

It's important to have your own credit history—a record of your payments on credit cards, charge accounts, installment loans, and mortgages kept by a credit bureau—in case your need money in a hurry or you are suddenly on your own. Using credit can prepare you for that unexpected need. This is not to suggest that you run up a big bill and pay off only part of it. But it is wise to build a credit record by judiciously using credit and paying your account promptly and in full when the bills arrive. You should use the card for at least three months out of twelve, paying it off each month, to establish a pattern of prompt payments.

Apply for a general purpose card, such as Visa or MasterCard, rather than a special purpose card such as those issued by department stores or mail order companies which usually charge higher interest on unpaid balances. Don't apply for more than one or two cards and don't apply for more than one at the same time. You see, every creditor who inquires about you will find out where else you have been applying for credit and for what amount.

When you marry, keep at least one or two credit cards in your first name and new married name but make sure these are under your own social security number.

If you want to avoid duplication, make sure at least one joint account has you listed as the person primarily responsible for paying the account. And again, be sure to use your social security number along with your first name, for example, Susan Smith, not Mrs. Robert Smith. Creditors must permit you to open and maintain credit accounts in your maiden name (if you retained it), in your first name and married surname or combined surname, whichever you prefer. For example, Susan Smith, Susan Jones, or Susan Smith-Jones.

If you plan to marry a man with a bad credit history, such as bankruptcy, keep your financial lives as separate as possible (yes, you should know his credit rating before you marry him). If his rating is bad, make all credit purchases in your own name and with your own accounts. Depending on the extent of your husband-to-be's credit problems, you could discover that you are more able to obtain financing for a home as a single than a married couple.

If you have a low income or are trying to reestablish credit after financial difficulties, try applying to your bank or local department store. If that fails, apply for a secured credit card using part of your savings as collateral. You will be required to make a deposit into the bank's savings account and can expect to pay higher interest rates and higher annual fees than on an unsecured card. But you will be reestablishing your credit, and that is what matters. I've attached a short list of banks with low-rate cards and also those who offer secured cards next to each is a space for you to write in their current rates and responses.

The Equal Credit Opportunity Act (ECOA) doesn't guarantee you credit, but it does prohibit discrimination on the basis of sex or marital status during any part of a credit transaction. Creditors must not discourage you from applying for credit because you're a woman, single or married, and they must not consider sex or marital status in any credit-scoring systems they use for evaluating credit-worthiness. Whether you're applying individually or with your husband, creditors cannot ask you about your plans or ability to have children, or about your birth-control practices. Creditors must not change the conditions of a credit account or close it solely because you get married or divorced, while you are contractually liable for it. However, you can be required to reapply for credit when your marital status changes, if credit was initially granted in part because of your husband's income.

Most credit card issuers want applicants to have a significant source of regular income, at least $15,000 a year is common, before they'll open an account. If you've been turned down by an issuer for lack of income, but have plenty of assets to tap, apply for a card at the bank or credit union where you normally do business. If you are rejected by an initial computerized evaluation, get a bank officer who knows your situation to make a request for special consideration. If you are at least 50 years old and a member of the American Association of Retired Persons (AARP), you can apply for a credit card issued through Bank One.

They will use worth rather than income as the basis for determining credit-worthiness. Membership in AARP is about $10 a year. The card carries a $10 annual fee and a variable interest rate. For more information call 1–800–283–3310.

Women who are or have been married are protected by another provisions as well. If you and your husband apply jointly for credit, creditors must consider your income, even if it is from a part-time job, in the same way they consider your husband's income, in determining your joint overall credit-worthiness and allowable credit limits. A creditor can not require a co-signor on your loan or credit account, unless the same requirement is imposed on all similarly qualified applicants. That is, others whose income, existing debt obligations, and credit history are comparable.

Women who are divorced get help from a provision that states that creditors must count as income any alimony or child-support payments, to the extent they are likely to continue (if you want them to). If you include these payments as income on a credit application, then the lender can ask for proof that the income is reliable. The lender is also entitled to check on your ex-husband's credit record if it is available. On the other hand, you do not have to disclose support income if you don't want to.

HOW MUCH DEBT CAN YOU HANDLE?

One long-standing rule of thumb is that monthly payments on consumer debt (credit card balances, car loans, and other borrowing, but not home mortgage) should not exceed 20% of your take-home pay. Most mortgage lenders will stipulate that your monthly housing payments (principal, interest, property taxes and home owners insurance—not private mortgage insurance) should not exceed 28% of your gross pay. When you add that payment to the rest of your installment debt, the figure should not exceed 33–40% (the average is 36%) of your gross monthly income.

WHERE DOES ALL THE MONEY GO?

If that question comes up in your home every week or so, I can try to help you answer it. But you'll have to do a little work. You see, before you can get ahead financially, you have to know where your "leaks" are. It's amazing how much money is spent on those little things throughout the day. A cup of coffee here, a magazine there. Before long you've spent $10 (if $10 doesn't seem like much, multiply it by 365 days a year and you're looking at a Hawaiian vacation). So here's what you do. Get a pocket calendar with enough space on each day to jot down those little cash outlays. You might be surprised at just how much you're spending that you could have saved.

If this measure doesn't seem like it's going be make much difference, you may have a larger problem. Many people overlook the signs because they don't want to admit that they are a high-risk candidate for financial trouble. Okay, you don't have to tell anyone if you have these symptoms. But if you do have any of these signs, review your spending habits and make some major changes, *now*!

* Always run to the bank or ATM to withdraw money

* Borrow from one credit card to pay down another

* Depleting saving accounts

* Drawing down lines of credit to live

* Excessive credit card debt

* Gambling (either for high stakes or often)

* Home-equity loans (excessive and frequent draw-downs)

* Never pay full balance on credit card bills

* Late monthly payments

* Negative balance in checking account

* Pledging belongings to pawn shops

* Second mortgage on house for no specific reason

* Selling belongings to get money

* Never have cash in your pocket

If any of these symptoms pertain to you, make sure you are taking every precaution to live within your means, and limit the amount of money available for discretionary items. It may be especially important for you to pay your bills automatically. In many cases, you can arrange with your local bank to have monthly wire transfers set up to pay your utility, telephone company, credit card companies and even your landlord or mortgage provider. Your local bank may even hold your mortgage. If so, have them take the payment directly from your checking account. You could also use this arrangement for autos loans. Although it may be difficult, please be honest with yourself. That's the only way things are going to get resolved in your financial future.

Credit card trouble is a serious situation which calls for drastic action. For your own well-being, don't spend more money on your credit cards than you can pay in full within 30 days. And, whatever you do, if you don't have a steady source of income, don't use your credit cards. If you can't control yourself with your credit cards just don't carry them at all. If you have accumulated huge balances on your credit cards, here are a few remedies to pay off the debt:

* Stop using your credit cards until you pay off the debt; cut them in half if necessary.

* Instead of spending more money on your credit cards, use the amount you budgeted for credit card spending to pay off the outstanding debt. This is why having a budget in the first place becomes so important. It allows you to correct things when they have gotten out of hand.

* Reduce the rate of interest being charged on your credit cards. This may mean contacting the card company (many of them will work with if you tell them your situation). Another option is to obtain a different card with a lower interest. The key here is to transfer the balance and cut up the old card.

* As a last resort, get a debt consolidation loan (make sure you consult with an accountant or financial advisor). And don't go to the shady ones, try your local bank or credit union first.

YOUR CREDIT REPORT:
KNOW YOUR RATING AND HOW TO DEAL WITH CREDIT BUREAUS

Credit histories are a fact of modern economic life. If you want a loan for a house or a car or the convenience of credit cards, someone is going to check your credit history. For this reason, it is critically important to verify on a regular basis that timely and accurate information is filed in your credit history.

Make it a practice to get a copy of your credit report every couple of years. At the very least, order one a few months before you apply for a mortgage. Knowing in advance how you look on paper and working to correct any inaccuracies is the best way to guard against a nasty credit surprise down the road. It is important also to check your credit rating after a divorce or the death of your spouse.

Your credit report is the key to your ability to access all the opportunities available to you as a consumer. If you want to ensure that you have as much credit-buying power at your fingertips as possible, you must be diligent about making sure that your credit report remains free of blemishes. Doing that requires you to become familiar with credit bureaus and, more importantly, how to interact with them properly so that as little negative information as possible remains on your credit report.

Contrary to popular belief, credit bureaus are not government agencies. Rather, they are private companies that have made it their business to maintain the credit histories of American citizens. Any potential grantors of credit (i.e., banks, retail stores, auto dealerships, credit card issuers, and so on) may, and likely do, subscribe to one or more of the three largest credit bureaus in the country.

Unfortunately, credit bureaus are notorious for making mistakes on the credit records of many people. They have no interest in self-policing and there is no other entity to police them. So, the job of making sure that your credit record remains accurate is yours alone. There are, however, a number of steps you can take to see that these bureaus keep your record as favorable as possible. On the following pages are several sample letters designed chiefly for use with the three largest credit bureaus. They are:

Equifax Information Service Center (may charge $8.00)
P.O. Box 4081
Atlanta, GA 30302
1–800–685–1111

Trans Union Corp. (may charge $8.00)
P.O. Box 7000
North Olmstead, OH 44070
East: 215–690–4955
Midwest: 312–408–1050
South: 502–425–7511
West: 714–738–3800
or 1–800–851–2674

TRW National Consumer Assistance Center (one free per year)
P.O. Box 2350
Chatsworth, CA 91313–2350
214–390–9191
or 1–800–392–1122

Should you ever find it necessary to send these facilities a letter, you will want to mail it via certified mail so you can be sure your correspondence is relieved and acknowledged. The industry standard practice has been to provide a free copy to anyone who has been denied credit within the past 60 days, provided you can furnish the bureau with a copy of the rejection letter. Otherwise, the cost per report can range from $2 to $16, depending on the bureau, your state of residence and whether the report is for an individual or a couple. TRW does offer one free copy per person, per year.

ADVICE FOR THOSE DROWNING IN DEBT:

You should inform your creditors of problems immediately. As I said before, they may be willing to work with you. Your next course of action, however, is to contact the nonprofit Consumer Credit Counseling Service. Counselors offer free budget planning and assistance in administering debt repayment. Call the National Foundation for Consumer Credit at 1–800–388–2227, or write them at 8611 Second Avenue, Suite 100, Silver Spring, MD 20910. Beware of firms advertising "quick fixes" or charging fees of $100 or more.

I also mentioned a debt consolidation loan and how it should be used as a last resort, however, if you use it carefully, it may help you dig your way out. You could consider a home equity loan because at least the interest could be tax deductible. Car loans pose a special problem because most financing agreements allow your car to be repossessed if the payments are not made. If they do repossess, the creditor will resell the car and you are still responsible for paying the difference of what you owe minus the selling price.

FILING FOR BANKRUPTCY:

Always get a second opinion before your file for bankruptcy. Unfortunately, some professionals prey upon people under this type of financial pressure. Bankruptcy is rarely in the best interest of the person considering it as an option. Be extremely careful with the information you receive.

There are two forms of personal bankruptcy: Chapter 13 and Chapter 7. Chapter 13 filing is usually preferable because it allows retention of personal property. To qualify under Chapter 13, you must owe less than $250,000 unsecured or $750,000 secured and have a regular income. The court will dictate that all or a portion of the debt be repaid over a period of three to five years.

The second and more severe from of bankruptcy is chapter 7. Filing this form asks the court to release you from your obligation to repay your debt. The court will most likely seize every asset within reach. However, if you do decide to file bankruptcy, you should consult a bankruptcy attorney about creditor-proof assets. Filing under Chapter 7 is a virtual guarantee that you will be denied credit for the next ten years.

A HOME AS AN INVESTMENT $\quad$ 8

The purchase of a home is one of your largest decisions. The need to own a home is a powerful motivating force (i.e., shelter is the base of Maslow's hierarchy of needs). For many women, however, the decision to buy a home has, thus far, usually been based on emotion with little or no cost-benefit analysis. Often we seem to focus most on this when we are newly married or a recent college graduate. This chapter will help you to answer the following important questions when considering a home:

1. Which strategy is better for you, renting or buying?

2. How much should you spend?

3. What questions need to be asked of the owner when buying a home?

4. How do you select a mortgage?

There was a time when home ownership was the epitome of the American Dream. The idea of being able to have a small piece of land that you could call your own has long been revered by many Americans. However, in recent years, home prices have either climbed out of reach or declined significantly. The volatility of the housing market has caused some women to question the wisdom of home ownership in the face of economically uncertain times. The question must be asked: Is home ownership still a worthwhile pursuit in light of the expenditures and risks involved?

Fortunately, home ownership is an intelligent step toward building net worth and should be regarded as a better option for most women. One big benefit of mortgage payments is that a mortgage is a systematic savings plan. Regular or "forced" savings combined with the tax deduction of mortgage interest are two of the reasons many women benefit from owning a home. Nonetheless, home ownership is not for everyone. Since a home is the biggest investment many women make, extreme care must be exercised to prevent a financial mistake that may take years to recover from.

We may never see homes appreciate as much as 15 to 20 percent per year as they did in the 1970s and 1980s, but it's still possible to get a rate of return that's comparable to a certificate of deposit or money market account. In many cases the actual return may be much higher. But, the key to understanding the value of home ownership is to have the proper perspective: Look at your home as a residence first and an investment second, not the other way around. As long as you are contemplating the purchase of a home with the intention of living in it for many years to come, you will be pleased with both the inner satisfaction you realize from owning your own residence as well as the financial satisfaction you'll realize years down the road.

There are however, some circumstances in which home ownership may not be a wise choice. If you believe you may not live in an area for long, renting may prove to be a better option. Also, if you live in rent-controlled housing where the monthly rent is far below what it would be elsewhere, renting may be smarter (in that case, you will want to invest the savings that you are realizing on your rent so that your money can grow).

HOW MUCH CAN YOU AFFORD?

Now that you have decided that home ownership may be the right choice. You need to know that your income and ability to meet mortgage payments are the key factors in determining how much you can borrow for a home. Most mortgage lenders require borrowers to meet specific income-to-expense ratios, commonly referred to as the 28/36 rule. I have mentioned this in a previous chapter but let's look at it again. Monthly mortgage payments (principal, interest, taxes and insurance also known as PITI) should not exceed 28% of your household's monthly gross income. Total monthly payments on all debt (with more than 10 monthly payments remaining), including your mortgage, should not exceed 36% of your gross income.

You can manipulate the rules several ways. For example, you could make a larger down payment, thus decreasing your monthly payments. Alternatively, you could pay off your car and credit card debts before applying for the home loan, which would allow you to spend 36% of gross income on a monthly mortgage payment. Most originators use these guidelines for qualifying prospective buyers. Lenders can not deny you a mortgage because you're a single woman or for other sex-based reasons. And if you're divorced, alimony and child-support payments count as income, if you want them to and if you can prove payments will continue for at least three years from the date of your loan application.

Most mortgage lenders want 10% to 20% of the price of a home as the down payment. If, however, your funds come up a bit short, find out if you are eligible for a loan guaranteed by the Federal Housing Administration (FHA) or the Department of Veterans Affairs(VA); both require little or no down payment. Also look into the 3/2 option loan. The Federal National Mortgage Association (FNMA—Fannie Mae) has a program designed for first-time buyers. The down payment must be at least 5%, and 3% of that must come from your own funds. You can use a gift or unsecured loan for up to 2% of the down payment. Check with your local bank or other mortgage lender to get the most up-to-date information.

You can also ask about obtaining private mortgage insurance (PMI). This is not the same insurance used in the calculation of PITI, however. With this type of insurance, your lender is more likely to give you a loan with less than 20% down, because they are protected if you should default on your loan and the price of your home has decreased, or they are simply not able to sell it for its full value. Private mortgage insurance can cost from $500 to $750 per year per $100,000 of mortgage loan. The less you have down, the more it will cost you until the equity in your home reaches 20%. A word of warning, however, many mortgage companies have been known to keep charging you the monthly fee for private mortgage insurance even after your equity has reached the 20% level. Be sure to watch this very closely.

You may also want to look into state and local programs to be able to get a lower-rate mortgage with a small down payment such as WHEDA. This is the Wisconsin Housing and Urban Development Authority. Lenders and real estate agents should know about these programs. Or you could contact the National Council of State Housing Agencies at 444 North Capital Street, NW, #438, Washington, D.C. 20001 or call 1–202–624–7710.

WHAT TYPE OF MORTGAGE IS BEST FOR YOU?

Once you have decided to purchase a home, the next most important decision is what type of mortgage you'll use to finance your purchase. If you do not select a mortgage with prudence and much forethought, the results may well affect whether or not you can enjoy your purchase. In extreme cases, the wrong mortgage can even cause you to lose your home.

There are two basic types of mortgages: fixed and variable. A fixed mortgage has an interest rate and monthly payment that stays the same throughout the life of the mortgage. With a variable mortgage, the rate you pay can (and probably will) change during the term of the mortgage as interest rates fluctuate. Fixed mortgages are the most popular because they give peace of mind to the buyer, who knows that the rate they settle on at the beginning will never change. Adjustable-rate mortgage costs will move in the same direction as interest rates, which means that your payments could go either up or down during the term of your mortgage. There can be good reasons to choose an adjustable-rate mortgage, but the uncertainty that comes with them makes them less popular overall.

Money lenders will use adjustable-rate mortgages to entice prospective home buyers into giving their loan business to them. They do this by offering the loan at an artificially low rate for the first year or two, with the understanding on the part of the buyer that the rate will increase as interest rates go up. For example, if the average lowest rate for a fixed mortgage is 8.25 percent, it's likely that you would be able to secure an adjustable-rate mortgage that requires you to pay about 7 percent for the first year or two. Some home buyers use these adjustables to get into a house that may be a bit out of their price range, but doing that can be dangerous. Should rates move upward, you might eventually find yourself with a monthly payment that you can't afford.

An adjustable-rate mortgage can be a good choice, but only under specific circumstances. If, for example, you choose to purchase a home even though you know you'll be there for only a few years, the adjustable rate would likely be the way to go. Then you can pay the artificially low rate, and when the payments begin to increase, you'll be on the way out. Also, if you opt for an adjustable mortgage at a time when interest rates are headed downward, your rate may very well decrease with them. Keep in mind that if you happen to have a fixed mortgage when rates go down, you can refinance the contract on your home to the new lower rate.

In summary, you need to be very certain that the terms of any adjustable-rate mortgage you're considering are more beneficial than the terms of any fixed-rate mortgage you might be eligible for. In other words, try to spend your time finding a fixed-rate mortgage, and if that doesn't work out, then go to the other options.

Renting Advantages	*Buying Advantages*
Renting is an excellent strategy to learn intricate details about the local area.	You are systematically saving for the future by building equity in your home.
Maintenance and yard work are the responsibility of the property owner.	The property may have appreciated in value when you wish to sell.
You have more time for relationships with friends, family, or pursuits like hobbies and travel. You may wish to use the extra time to invest in yourself, thereby increasing your ability to earn income.	Home equity can be a souce of emergency funds.
	Taxes from the sale of your home may be deferred if you buy a more expensive home within two years.
The money that you would have used for a down payment may be more profitably invested elsewhere.	Mortgage interest payments and property taxes are deductible.
The risk of real-estate devaluation is avoided when you wish to move.	Rent increases and landlord negotiations are avoided.
You have more freedom to seize new career opportunities or take greater risks.	A portion or all of your home can serve as a source of rental income.
Heat, some utilities, and major appliances may be provided by the property owner. Property taxes and mortgage interest are avoided.	You have more freedom to have animals or change your property.
	You have pride of ownership.
In rent-controlled areas, you may find exceptional bargains.	You may find an exceptional buy.

School selection, commuting distance to work, and many other important variables need to be considered when comparing specific property.

RISK MANAGEMENT/INSURANCE

9

Insurance is the most widely used method of managing the possibility of loss. The term "Risk Management" means that you use various ways to deal with potential personal or financial loss. If you use risk management, it means you recognize the existence and impact of potential losses.

If you've ever taken one of the "stress tests" published in popular magazines, you probably learned that the root of your stress was tied to some type of life-changing event, and there's no doubt about it, stress is part of life. While I'm not in the business of giving personal advice on dealing with changes in your life, I think I can help you with another consequence of change: stressed-out insurance. If any of these events have happened since you last reviewed your life insurance coverage, it's time to re-examine your life insurance needs:

* Change in your marital status

* Additional children joining your family (born or adopted)

* Children completing their education or leaving home

* Promotion at work

* Job or career change

* Home purchase

* Separation from the military

*   Retirement

If you answered "yes" to one or more of the above events, you need to speak to someone who will take the time to review your insurance needs. The best way to determine exactly how much life insurance you need is to request a needs analysis from a qualified professional.

Marriage, divorce or the death of a spouse—gaining or losing a partner is a major life event. Whether for better or worse, marriage usually expands your financial obligations such as credit card debt, car and student loans, a mortgage, child care expenses and more. You and your spouse can start your financial planning by looking at your life insurance, beginning with whatever each of you has in force now. If you both work, you may already have some kind of coverage, probably a group policy through your employer. Check to see what kind of coverage it is, how much you have, and its limitations.

Then list all your financial obligations to come up with a rough idea of how much insurance you need. Now is also the time to be sure your policy is updated with your new address, if you've moved, and any change in beneficiary you may wish to make.

At this point, you and your spouse need to ask yourselves some hard questions. If one partner died, could the other continue to meet all obligations on one income? If you own a home together, could you afford to meet the monthly payments on one income alone? Probably not, if both of your incomes were necessary to qualify for a loan in the first place. That's a sure sign you'd need to replace the lost income or pay off the mortgage in the event of a partner's death.

If you've recently gone through a divorce, you may no longer be responsible for some of your former spouse's financial obligations. If this is the case, you may want to reduce the amount of your insurance to an amount sufficient to meet your new obligations and goals. You may also need or want to change the name of your beneficiary.

But if you have young children, it's a good idea to carry enough life insurance to provide for their education and well-being. If they aren't protected by the other parent's coverage, a policy on your life could provide benefits for them in case of your death. Something to remember also: A spouse receiving child support may need a special decree from the court to ensure that children will continue to receive support if the other parent should die.

A new baby is a life event that can turn your entire life insurance perspective around. Considering the cost of raising a child to adulthood with child care, education, clothing, doctor's visits and all the other everyday living expenses, you can see why it's important to carry sufficient insurance to help meet children's needs in the event of a parent's untimely death.

If your life insurance is centered around getting your children through college, then your objective may be accomplished when they leave home to start their own families and careers. This is a good time for you and your spouse to re-evaluate what you want to accomplish and then tailor your life insurance around your new goals. You may find yourself converting your present policy to another type, especially if you have a term policy with increasing premiums or one that doesn't last beyond age 70. Or you may want to reduce the amount of your coverage. Discussing your needs with an experienced professional can help you zero in on the amount of insurance you need.

When you retire, you could find yourself in one of two financial positions: on track or off the track. If you're on track, with sufficient income from several sources, your only real need for life insurance may be to pay final expenses or to leave money to your children or grandchildren. If you've done really well, you probably will have estate planning needs that make life insurance a top priority.

On the other hand, if your financial planning for retirement has taken a detour from the main road, you may need to supplement your income after you retire. In the event of your death, you may want to provide an adequate income for your surviving spouse or pay off the mortgage or any other financial obligations you may have.

As you can see, any of the life events discussed above can have a significant impact on your need for life insurance, and everyone needs a financial safety net. The question is, how big should it be? As a rule of thumb, you should give your life insurance a checkup every two to three years just to make sure it's still adequate to meet your ever-changing needs. A single woman, for example, with no other debts may need no insurance on her life. While a single mother, as her family's main breadwinner, needs a lot. A full-time homemaker may depend heavily on her husband's policy. At the same time he may need life insurance on her if paying a care-giver to replace her would be a financial hardship.

Many people are unclear as to whether or not they have adequate life insurance. A good way to determine your insurance need is to determine the amount, if invested wisely, that would continue your income for your family. You should also consider your family's cash needs in the event of your death. For a truly accurate figure, however, you will need to adjust for inflation and figure the present value of a future need. A well-qualified financial advisor can help you.

Your personal life insurance is a very important decision for you to be comfortable with. I could tell you that you needed 10 or 15 times your current annual salary just to start with. That doesn't make it a correct number for you and your family. On the following pages are explanations of the major types of life insurance. An overall risk management plan should be build on a solid foundation. Life, Property, Liability, and Disability Insurance should all be viewed as basic ingredients, or the foundation of your financial plan. A disabling accident, property loss, or unforeseen liabilities can put significant cracks in your plan. This could result in you and your family having to alter your long-term goals and lower your expectations.

The total, permanent disability or death of a spouse is never easy to handle. Yet, planning and foresight can help your family avoid unreasonable and unrealistic financial demands. Adequate life insurance can assure that your years of work and successful financial planning can continue to be part of your family's long-term goals.

METHODS OF HANDLING RISK

* Risk Acceptance—choosing to bear the full financial burden yourself in the event of loss.

* The Use of Deductibles—the sharing of risk, that is, you are responsible for losses incurred up to a specified dollar amount; then the insurance company pays for damages above the deductible amount.

* Avoidance—removing the possibility of loss by deciding not to partic-ipate in the risk-creating activity. Reduction—minimizing the possibility of loss through restricting the conditions that create loss.

* Transfer Risk—the purchasing of insurance to cover any loss incurred. (See the Glossary in the back of this book for many other helpful terms.)

AREAS OF RISK MANAGEMENT INCLUDE:

Life Insurance—To handle risk of premature death*
There are three basic reasons for life insurance in traditional family planning to cover any premature death. Those are:

1. Replacement of income (either yours or your spouse's)

2. Debt Reduction

3. College funds for children (or yourself)

Health Insurance—For medical and catastrophic injury expenses

Disability Insurance—Insuring against the loss of income in the event of an injury

Long-term Care Insurance—For Nursing, Home Health Care and Adult Day Care

Property Insurance—To cover financial loss when property is damaged

Liability Insurance— "Creditor Proof" umbrella insurance. Protection from lawsuits

Auto and Home—Can also be property and liability insurance
Business planning, however, also needs to be considered in your overall life insurance decision. These elements are as follows:

1. Buy-Sell Funding

2. Non-qualified Retirement Planning

3. Key Person Coverage

4. Debt Reduction

Finally, whether you own a business or not, you will probably need insurance for your estate planning needs. These could most likely include:

1. Reducing estate taxes with gifting programs

2. Multiply estate value with lump sum deposit

3. Replace IRA taxes at death

4. Provide maximum investment yield (tax-free)

THERE ARE BASICALLY THREE MAJOR TYPES OF LIFE INSURANCE:

Term Insurance—This is the equivalent of "renting" insurance. It has NO cash value and coverage stops as soon as you stop making payments. This is usually very low-cost and is primarily used when young families have children to support and smaller incomes or with business owners who have a large debt responsibility and their cash flow is not sufficient for permanent insurance.

Whole Life Insurance—Typically referred to as permanent or traditional cash value life insurance, this type offers guaranteed death benefits, cash values, level premiums and possibly dividends. This form can be an efficient method of purchasing insurance on a long-term basis. Cash values are created by insurance company investment of excess premiums in a long-term portfolio with legal reserve requirements. The most basic form of this type of policy is referred to as "Ordinary" or "Straight" life.

Universal Life Insurance—Universal Life Insurance was created with flexibility in mind. Both premium payments and death benefits may be varied, within limits, to meet your needs. This contemporary financial planning product was built on the foundation of low-cost term combined with a tax-sheltered annuity earning variable rates of return. As the policy owner pays premiums, a portion is used to pay for the pure term insurance rates and the balance is deposited into a side fund upon which interest is paid. If the premium paid is not sufficient to cover the cost of the term insurance, the balance is taken out of the side fund. The policy owner may elect to vary the premiums upward or downward, subject to some limits.

The policy owner may also choose to skip premium payments without losing insurance coverage if there is adequate accumulated values in the savings portion of the contract. You may choose to invest these side funds into mutual fund investments.

THE MONEY FLOW   **10**

The money that powers our economy is created essentially out of nothing by the Federal Reserve. Keeping a modern economy running smoothly requires a pilot who will keep it from stalling or accelerating too fast. The United States, like most other countries, tries to control the amount of money in circulation. The process of injecting or withdrawing money reflects the monetary policy that the Federal Reserve adopts to regulate the economy.

Monetary policy isn't a fixed ideology. It's a constant juggling act to keep enough money in the economy so that it flourishes without growing too fast. But how does it actually work, you ask? Let's examine it further.

The Federal Reserve's Open Market Committee meets about every six weeks to evaluate the economy. Then it tells the Federal Reserve Bank of New York (the city where the nation's biggest banks and brokerage firms have their headquarters) whether to speed up or slow down the creation of new money.

About 11:15 a.m. E.S.T. (Eastern Standard Time) every day, the New York Federal Reserve Bank decides whether to withdraw money from the economy, or inject some, in order to implement the Open Market Committee's policy decision. Also, the Federal Reserve requires that all banks keep a portion, usually 10%, of their deposits in a fund to cover any unusual demand from customers for cash. For all practical purposes, there isn't any limit on the amount of money the Federal Reserve can create. The $100 million example here is only a modest increase in the money supply. In a typical month, the Fed might pump as much as $4 billion or as little as $1 billion into the economy. You see, to create money, the New York Fed buys government securities from banks and brokerage houses. The money that pays for the securities has not existed before, but it has value, or worth, because the securities the Fed has purchased with it are valuable. More new money is created when the banks and brokers lend the money they receive from selling the securities to clients or customers who in turn spend it on goods and services.

To slow down an economy where too much money is in circulation, the New York Federal Reserve sells government securities, taking in the cash that would otherwise be available for lending. In its role as banker to banks, the Fed can also influence the amount of money in circulation by changing the interest rate, called the discount rate, it charges banks to borrow money. If the discount rate is high, banks are discouraged from borrowing. If the discount rate is low, banks borrow more freely, and lend money to their clients more freely.

It isn't easy to regulate the money supply or control the rate of growth. That's because the economy doesn't always respond quickly or precisely when the Fed acts. Typically, it takes about six months for significant policy changes to affect the economy directly. That lag helps explain why the economy seems to have a life of its own, growing too much in some years and not enough in others.

According to the Humphrey Hawkins Act of 1978, the Fed has to announce its targets for monetary growth every six months. But it isn't required to meet the goals, and can change direction or policy if it wants to.

MEASURING ECONOMIC HEALTH

Economists keep their fingers on the pulse of the economy at all times, determined to cure what ails it. Intensive care is a 24-hour business. Doctors and nurses measure vital signs, record changes in temperature and physical functions, conduct test after test. That gives you an idea of how thousands of experts, and countless more interested amateurs, watch the economy.

The biggest differences? The vigil never stops—even when the economy seems to be healthy. There's no consensus on how to cure what ails the patient when the vital signs are poor.

So, what do they measure?

Jobless Claims—

New unemployment claims for state unemployment insurance give a sense of the number of people losing their jobs. A falling number is a sign the economy is growing. For example, the improvement in late 1992 didn't signal a full recovery, as the jobless claims climbed again in 1993.

Durable Goods—

A backlog on orders for a wide range of products, from aircraft to home appliances, signals increased demand that will keep the economy expanding. Since late 1990, there has been erratic movement, suggesting that consumers were getting and giving mixed signals about the financial future.

Housing Starts—

The number of building permits being issued is a measure of economic health. A growing economy generates increased demand for new housing. This chart shows a low in January 1991 and a period of ups and downs in 1993. Since 1995, housing has remained fairly strong, as has the economy in general.

HAVE YOU EVER WONDERED WHY ECONOMIC INDICATORS ARE SO IMPORTANT?

The Index of Leading Economic Indicators is released every month by the U.S. Commerce Department. It tracks the performance of the economy by measuring changes in the business cycle (the alternating progression of the economy from periods of expansion, when business is growing, to periods of contraction, when business activity slows and unemployment increases). Leading indicators are those factors that have shown the tendency to signal change before the economy makes a major turn. The index measures changes in such factors as stock prices, contracts and orders for plants, and equipment, the M2 money supply (includes all money in immediately spendable forms such as cash, checking and savings accounts, as well as that in certificate of deposits or CDs. The latter can't be spent directly, but can be converted easily into cash). The index also includes those indicators shown above.

Gross Domestic Product (GDP) measures the final output of goods and services produced in the United States in one year, which makes it the broadest measure of economic performance. Initial estimates are released about a month after the close of each quarter. Financial markets react strongly to the GDP number because it indicates the pace of economic activity. For instance, if the GDP is growing at a faster pace than the previous periods, it's an indication that the economy may be heating up. Rapid growth strains the economy, and that drives up prices and interest rates. The resulting inflation erodes corporate profits and the value of financial securities. Conversely, growth that is too slow causes prices and profits to fall, and that drives up unemployment and dries up demand.

Monthly industrial production and capacity indicators report the efficiency of economic productivity. The index of industrial production measures changes in the output of the mining, manufacturing, and gas and electric utilities sectors of the economy. Capacity utilization is the rate at which industrial production sectors operate (it is an indicator of industry's current physical limits).

All of these indicators together provide a simple way to keep an eye on the economy's health. Generally, three consecutive rises in the Index are considered a sign that the economy is growing (that would mean, of course, that three drops mean a sign of decline). Eleven leading indicators are averaged to produce the Index. They include the four listed on the previous page, plus monthly averages of stock prices, the M2 Money Supply and several measures of manufacturing performance, like the average weekly hours worked.

INFLATION AND THE EVER-INCREASING COST OF LIVING

11

Women always tell me they're concerned about risk, which they define as "losing their money." Actually, the biggest risk that women face is the loss of purchasing power. I'm taking about inflation, the biggest obstacle investors face, especially women, because they live longer. We need to ensure that the money we work so hard to accumulate isn't eroded by the rising cost of living. Nobody can predict the future, but very few people think anything (housing, college tuition, or groceries) will cost less 10 years from now. The big problem with inflation is that it's invisible. We all can watch the nightly news to find out how the stock market did, but no one is telling us on a regular basis how the purchasing power of a dollar is shrinking.

Over the last twenty years, the cost of a college education has more than tripled. The cost of a new home has done the same. And automobiles? They now cost more than four times what they did in 1976! All in all, one dollar twenty years ago is only worth 31 cents today.

Inflation is an economic given. It always has, and always will, erode your purchasing power. CDs and savings accounts may be good short-term savings vehicles for a portion of your assets because they offer safety of principal and a guaranteed rate of return. Unfortunately, they simply might not provide enough income over the long haul. To maintain your standard of living over time, your investments must out pace inflation.

Simply put, inflation decreases the purchasing power of your savings by inflating the cost of what you buy. In 20 years, a 4% rate of inflation will reduce the buying power of a dollar by more than half. That's why it is so important that your investments bring in a total return greater than the effects of inflation. Otherwise, the purchasing power of your investments may actually decrease over time, due to the impact of inflation on the costs of goods and services you buy.

Conservative savings vehicles such as Treasury Bills and CDs tend to fluctuate less than equities. But historically, they've often struggled to keep pace with the rate of inflation. That's why it is important to look at the "real returns"—annual returns minus inflation. If your real returns do not increase, neither does your purchasing power. Keep in mind, however, CDs offer a guaranteed return of principal over a stated period of time and a fixed rate of interest. They are typically issued by institutions whose deposits are insured.

Inflation and recession are recurring phases of a continuous economic cycle. Experts work hard to predict their timing and control their effects. Inflation occurs when prices rise because there's too much money in circulation and not enough goods and services to spend it on. When prices go higher than people can—or will—pay, demand decreases and a downturn begins.

Modern economics don't let the economic cycle run unchecked, because the consequences could be a major worldwide depression like the one that followed the stock market crash of 1929. In a depression, money is so tight that the economy virtually grinds to a halt, unemployment escalates, businesses collapse and the general outlook is grim.

Instead, governments and central banks change their monetary policy, as discussed in the previous chapter, to affect what's happening in the economy. In a recession, the Fed can create new money to make borrowing easier. As the economy picks up, sellers sense rising demand for their products or services and begin to raise prices. That's inflation!

The rule of 72 is a reliable guide to the impact of inflation. It's based on dividing 72 by the number of years it will take prices to double. For example, when inflation is at 10%, prices will double in 7 years ($72 \div 10 = 7$) and when it's 4% they will double in 18 years ($72 \div 4 = 18$).

Most economists agree that inflation isn't good for the economy because, over time, it destroys value, including the value of money. Inflation also prompts investors to buy things they can resell at huge profits (like art or real estate) rather than putting their money into companies that can create new products and jobs.

Inflation is often the result of political pressures. A growing economy creates jobs and reduces unemployment. Politicians are almost always in favor of that, so they urge the Federal Reserve to adopt an easy money policy that stimulates the economy. The most effective method for ending inflation is for the Fed to induce a recession, or downturn, in the economy (two consecutive quarters in which the economy shrinks is considered a recession). To avert long-term slowdowns or the more serious problem of a depression, politicians and the Fed, once they observe that the economy is beginning to shrink, reverse their policies to stimulate more borrowing and economic growth. In time, the country emerges from recession, begins growing, and the completed cycle begins anew.

MARKET INDEXES   **12**

The Dow Jones Industrial Average traces more than the development of American business from small, local companies into global powerhouses. It chronicles the evolution of investing as well. When Charles H. Dow first unveiled his industrial-stock average on May 26, 1896, the stock market wasn't highly regarded. Prudent investors bought bonds, which paid predictable amounts of interest and were backed by machinery, buildings and other hard assets.

Stocks, by contrast, were considered very unsavory because daredevil speculators, conniving Wall Street pool operators and corporate raiders did their best to stage manage prices. Stocks moved on dubious tips and scurrilous gossip because solid information was hard to come by.

Today, stocks are routinely considered as investment vehicles, even by conservative investors. Interest has widened far beyond the Wall Street cliques of the past century to millions of everyday women, like yourself, who turn to stocks to help them amass capital for their children's college tuition bills and your own retirement. The Dow Jones Industrial Average played a role in bringing about this tremendous change.

In 1896, even people on Wall Street found it hard to tell from the daily jumble of up-a-quarter and down-an-eighth whether stocks generally were rising, falling or treading water. Charles Dow devised his stock average to make sense out of this confusion.

He began in 1884 with 11 stocks, most of them railroads—the first great national corporations. He compared his average to placing sticks in beach sand to determine, wave after successive wave, whether the tide was coming in or going out. If the average's peaks and troughs rose progressively higher, a bull market prevailed; if the peaks and troughs dropped lower and lower, a bear market was on.

This seems simplistic in these days of myriad market indicators, but late in the eighteenth century, Mr. Dow's average was a powerful new beacon that cut through the fog. It provided a convenient benchmark for comparing individual stocks to the course of the market, for comparing the market with other economic indicators, or simply for conversation at the corner of Wall and Broad Streets about the market's direction.

The stock average was just one expression of the mission Mr. Dow and his partners, Edward D. Jones and Charles M. Bergstresser, set for themselves in founding Dow Jones & Company in 1881: to enlighten investors and business people with accurate, factual information, speedily delivered. By tending resolutely to this purpose, the fledgling company built a reputation for integrity.

Though they had nothing to do with the averages directly, Mr. Jones and Mr. Bergstresser contributed immensely to the environment in which Mr. Dow nurtured his creations. The mechanics of the first stock average were dictated by the necessity of computing it with pencil and paper: add up the prices and divide by the number of stocks. This application of grade-school arithmetic, while creative, is hardly worthy of remembrance a century later. But the very idea of using an index to differentiate the stock market's long-term fluctuations deserves a salute. Without the means for ordinary investors to follow the market, today's age of financial democracy—in which millions of employees actively direct the investment of their own pension money and as a result are substantial share-holders—would be unimaginable.

Following the introduction of the industrial average, Mr. Dow modified his original index, begun 12 years earlier, to create a 20-stock railroad average. It was renamed the transportation average in 1970. The Dow Jones Utilities Average came along in 1929, more than 25 years after Charles Dow's death at age 51 in 1902.

At first, the industrial average was published irregularly, but daily publication in the *Wall Street Journal* began on October 7, 1896. In 1916, the average was expanded to 20 stocks: that number of stocks rose again in 1928 to 30, where it remains. Also in 1928, the editors of the *Journal* began calculating the average with a special divisor other than the number of stocks, to avoid distortions when constituent companies split their shares or when one stock was substituted for another. Through habit, this index was still identified as an "average."

Mr. Dow perceived well ahead of the crowd that America's industrial sector was emerging as a distinct part of the economy and that it would be of interest to investors, his readers. There is no indication in his *Journal* editorials that Mr. Dow foresaw the rise of the greatest industrial power in the world, and the tall, taciturn journalist left hardly any personal records that might reveal his private thoughts.

But he was acutely conscious of the rhythms of economic life because they lived when prosperity was regularly cut short by recessions and panics.

No single index can tell investors everything they need, or want, to know about the stock market. There are, however, indexes to track practically everything.

The **Dow Jones Industrial Average** is composed of 30 large capitalized, blue-chip, major industrial companies, which are worth about 25% of the total value of all stocks listed on the New York Stock Exchange. The "Dow" is the oldest index and probably the most well known gauge of stock performance.

The 30 stocks on this index are:

AT&T (T)	Eastman Kodak (EK)	Merek & Co. (MRK)
Allied-Signal (ALD)	Exxon Corp. (XON)	Minn. Mining & Mfg (MMM)
Aluminum Company of America (AA)	General Electric (GE)	JP Morgan (JPM)
American Express (AXP)	General Motors (GM)	Philip Morris (MO)
Boeing Company (BA)	Goodyear Tire (GT)	Proctor & Gamble (PG)
Caterpillar (CAT)	Hewlett Packard (HWP)	Sears, Roebuck & Co. (S)
Chevron Corp. (CHV)	Intn'l Bus. Mach (IBM)	Travelers Group (TRV)
Coca Cola (KO)	International Paper (IP)	Union Carbide (UK)

Walt Disney Co. (DIS)	Johnson & Johnson (JNJ)	United Technologies (UTX)
Du Pont (DD)	McDonalds (MCD)	Walmart (WMT)

The Dow Jones Industrial Average is just that, an average, please keep in mind that it is only these 30 stocks. It revered by our society as the index to watch, but it is only a measure of these large companies. When you are deciding upon investments. You need to be aware of this as a point of interest. This is, however, not the only index and not the only piece of your investment puzzle.

Other indexes include the **Standard & Poor's 500 Composite Stock Price Index** (S&P). The origins of the S&P 500 Index go back to 1923 when Standard & Poor's introduced a series of indices which included 233 companies and covered 26 industries. The index as it is now known was introduced in 1957. Today, the S&P 500 encompasses 500 companies representing 90 specific industry groups.

There are three groupings or classifications that you also need to be aware of. These are the "large-caps," the "mid-caps" and the "small-caps." The large-caps refer to those stocks that have a market capitalization of $5 billion or more. The mid-caps are those between $5 billion and $1 billion and the small-caps are those with a market capitalization of $1 billion or less. Some analysts refer to small-caps as those $2 billion or less. To determine capitalization, you take the price of the stock times the amount of share outstanding. You can find the amount of shares outstanding in the company's annual report or from an investment professional. You can also find this information in reports such as "Value Line" or "Morningstar." These are independent reporting firms that only provide information about publicly held companies, they do not give investment advice.

Automatic Data Processing (ADP) disseminates S&P 500 Index values every 15 seconds during the trading day. ADP also transmits Index values to the Chicago Mercantile Exchange, where S&P 500 futures trade, and the Chicago Board Options Exchange, home of the S&P 500 Options. The exchanges in turn distribute the Index values to numerous quotation vendors. This insures the widest possible means of distribution. The S&P 500 Index is reported daily in the *Wall Street Journal*, the *New York Times*, *U.S.A. Today*, and virtually every major regional and local newspaper. The "500" is also reported on most television and radio business programs.

The S&P Index Committee is responsible for establishing index policy. The management of the S&P 500 Index is totally objective and independent from S&P's other business operations and interests. Even though the "Dow" is the oldest, the S&P 500 Index is widely regarded as the standard for broad stock market performance.

This index includes a representative sample of common stocks traded on the New York Stock Exchange, American Stock Exchange and NASDAQ National Market System. It has, since 1968, also been one of the U.S. Commerce Department's leading indicators. The S&P represents over 70% of the total domestic U.S. equity market capitalization and is divided thus: 400 industrial companies, 20 transportation companies, 40 utilities and 40 financial companies.

Two other less well known indices are:

The **Russell 2000** which represents the smallest two-thirds of the 3,000 largest U.S. companies, including a great many of the initial public offerings of the last few years.

The **Wilshire 5000**, the broadest index, monitors 5,000 stocks traded on the NASDAQ and the exchanges.

RISK CAN HAVE ITS REWARDS

13

Successful investing takes into account the interplay of risk as well as time. Seasoned investors know that time can be used to help diminish the impact or risk, since, over time, the effects of short-term volatility may be less important than the potential for higher returns available when investing for the long-term. There is often a risk-reward trade-off, in that investors must be willing to assume additional risk when making investments (such as aggressive growth investments) to seek higher returns. You should understand that if you allow risk avoidance to dominate your investment strategy, you become subject to the risk that the earnings on your investment, when reduced by inflation, provide little opportunity for you to ever achieve your investment objectives. In short, there is no such thing as a "risk-free" investment strategy.

Your specific goals will dictate your priorities. Occasionally, simultaneous goals result in confusion and indecision. I hope the financial pyramid shown on the following page helps you decide what action to take first. In a given situation, certain financial products will be more important than others. For instance, if you do not own health insurance and are given a choice of buying health insurance or investment art, you would choose health insurance. Common sense dictates that the need for health insurance is more important than buying art. The same logic can be applied to any situation you are faced with.

A well-designed financial plan will first identify where you are now and where you want to be in the future. We have already begun with the Profile Questionnaire in Chapter 4. After determining cash flow, the foundation of your financial future must be established. This is the written plan that includes goals for the short-term (0 to 3 years), the mid-term (3 to 7 years) and the long-term (7+ years) as well as your budget for the entire next year. Subsequent layers of your financial pyramid will then be built on a solid lower layer, ensuring a secure structure.

Imagine the person who buys 1,000 shares of ABC stock without first establishing an emergency fund. The decision to sell shares of ABC will now be dependent on when the car breaks down or some other financial crisis arises.

The financial hierarchy philosophy is based on the fact that the risk of death, accident, sickness, or disability can cause a financial disaster at any moment. Therefore, the core elements of your financial foundation must be addressed prior to investing in stocks, bonds, real estate, or even mutual funds. The key point to remember about insurance is that you must buy it before you need it. When you need insurance because you have already suffered a loss, you cannot buy it. Another key point is that insurance is risk management, not an investment. You may use it to strategically provide for your needs in the future, but you must always remember that you buy it for protection.

TIME, NOT TIMING, IS THE ONE IMPORTANT KEY

As investors, you are inundated with newspapers, magazines, newsletters, and mailings all talking about whether the stock market is too high or too low and whether you should buy or sell. It is tempting to try and find the "perfect" time to buy into a rally or sell before a loss. History shows, however, that moving in and out of the stock market in order to minimize losses and maximize gains is a sure money loser.

Using the S&P 500 Index that we have just reviewed in the previous chapter as a proxy for the stock market, look what would happen if you stayed fully invested compared to if, in an attempt to time the market, you missed the 10 best days or more on Wall Street in the past 10 years.

THE S&P 500 INDEX (12/31/19–12/31/96)

Days Missed	Annualized Total Return	
None	15.27%	(Past performance is
Best 10 days	7.77%	not indicative of future
Best 20 days	4.85%	results)
Best 30 days	2.37%	
Best 40 days	0.09%	

In times of market volatility it may be difficult to stick with your investing program. You may not realize, though, that the best and worst days come exactly at times of market volatility. For example, the worst one-day decline in the Dow Jones Industrial Average was October 19, 1987, when it fell 508 points. The best one-day gain in the Dow was two days later on October 21, when it gained 186.84 points.

TIPS FOR KEEPING A LEVEL HEAD

Given the erratic behavior of the market in recent months, you may be tempted to tinker with your portfolio in an attempt to avoid a downturn. Your best bet, though, is to develop a long-term plan and stick with it. Here are six time-tested strategies that have served investors well. These strategies can help to smooth out the impact of market fluctuations over time as well as potentially enhance overall performance results. I hope these will help you to "keep a level head" during periods of uncertainty.

1. *Ignore short-term static:*

   The best thing to do is to forget the day-to-day gyrations of the market. Your investments may experience substantial swings in value over short time periods, as indicated in the graph below. In order to comfortably absorb these fluctuations, you should make sure that your portfolio's assets are allocated appropriately among the investment levels shown in the financial investment pyramid, according to your time horizon and risk tolerance. Unless you are nearing the point at which you will be withdrawing your retirement funds, it's better to have a long-term perspective.

The variability of average annual returns over long periods of time is much less than over shorter periods.

2. *Use Asset Allocation to achieve your goals:*

    Asset allocation seeks to spread the risk of investing by apportioning your investments over different categories (or types) of investments instead of choosing a single investment category, while capitalizing on potential high growth areas. Allocating your assets across a spectrum can help provide an effective way of building an investment portfolio. The benefits of asset allocation can be summed up in a single word: diversification. By diversifying your savings across different types of investments, asset allocation helps reduce the risk of volatility associated with any one particular investment or investment category. The advantages of asset allocation include the ability to tailor your investment portfolio to your individual needs, while participating in a wide spectrum of investments that offer goals ranging from protection of your principal to achieving substantial growth over time.

3. *Don't Panic / Don't Time the Market:*

    Perhaps the most compelling reason to keep your holdings during a market decline is this: Your portfolio will be positioned to reap gains as the market recovers. If you panic, though, you are likely to miss out on the early stages of the next bull market—forever. Indeed, as the information at the bottom of page 94 indicated, it is far more costly to miss out on bull markets than to endure a bear market.

4. *The Potential of Systematic Investing:*

    Dollar-Cost Averaging: Sleeping through weather Fair or Foul

    The motto says "buy low and sell high," but it's easy for an investor to buy high and sell low instead. When markets are rising, the temptation to get in on the action can be irresistible. When markets are dropping, people naturally want to cut their losses and get out while the getting is good. And then there are markets like this year's (1998), when many observers are advising caution and the market indicators are decidedly mixed. Is there a way to enjoy the advantages of having investments and still get a good night's sleep?

Dollar-Cost Averaging Employs Discipline, Not Emotion!

With dollar-cost averaging, you invest a set amount of money at regular intervals regardless of the market swings or pundits' forecasts. You decide how much and how often to invest. And you decide when to change the amount or the schedule if doing so suits your investment strategies.

Here's an example: $200 investment per month*

Month	Net Asset Value	# of shares purchased
January	$ 24.00	8.333
February	$ 20.00	10.000
March	$ 14.00	14.286
April	$ 18.00	11.111
May	$ 22.00	9.090
June	$ 24.00	8.333

Average Net Asset Value: $ 20.33
Total shares Bought: 61.153
Average purchase price per share: $ 19.62

You save about $. 70 cents per share

* These results are hypothetical

THIS TECHNIQUE HAS EMOTIONAL ADVANTAGES

You will be less tempted to make investment decisions on the basis of short-term phenomena and your feelings of the moment.

Whichever way the market is moving, you will be part of it. Your fortunes as an investor won't depend entirely on your making a right call about future trends.

LIKE EVERY FINANCIAL TECHNIQUE, WE NEED TO LOOK ALSO AT THE FINANCIAL DISADVANTAGES

You automatically purchase fewer shares of the mutual fund when its cost per share is high.

DON'T DOLLAR-COST AVERAGE ALL YOUR MONEY!

The technique is especially appropriate to investments where your goals are long-term, since over time market volatility tends to even itself out. Dollar-cost averaging involves investing continuously regardless of fluctuating securities prices, so you need to be confident that you can keep making purchases for an extended period. No investment technique can assure a profit in a declining market. What dollar-cost averaging will do is apply discipline to your investing behavior, discipline that can be especially important when market watchers issue conflicting forecasts.

5. *Use Mutual Funds:*

   Not everybody has the time or expertise to analyze individual stocks and bonds. Mutual funds may offer you an easier way to invest for your future. In a mutual fund, your money is pooled with other people's money. A professional manager invests for you, seeking to achieve diversification within each fund's specific goals—whether it's to generate monthly income, long-term growth, or something in between. In Chapter 13, I continue with a detailed discussion of mutual funds.

6. *Consult an Investment Professional:*

   With so many mutual funds and companies to choose from, seeking the advice of a qualified investment professional may be one of the smartest decisions you make. An investment professional can help you define your personal goals and tolerance for risk, recommend a strategy, and monitor the performance of your investments.

   A successful long-term investment strategy is a process that evolves as your needs and goals change and grow for each new point in your life. Remember what I always say: "Life Happens." An experienced investment advisor can be invaluable in helping you take stock of where you are and where you'd like to be in 5, 10, or even 30 years. With more than 8,000 mutual fund choices available today, not to mention all the common and preferred stocks as well as the countless bond choices, your advisor can also help you wade through all the choices, to find those that are right for you.

As the years go by, and your circumstances change, you can depend on your advisor for continuing informed advice. And very importantly, you can look to your advisor to help you avoid making rash investment decisions in volatile markets.

THE FUNDAMENTALS OF MUTUAL FUNDS

14

A mutual fund is an investment company that makes investments on behalf of investors sharing common financial goals. A mutual fund pools the money of many people having similar investment objectives, each with a different amount to invest. Professional money managers employed by the fund use the pool of money to buy a wide range of stocks, bonds, or money market instruments that, in their judgment, will help the fund's shareholders achieve their financial objectives.

Each fund has a financial objective (it's described in the fund's prospectus), which is important to both the manager and the portfolio investor (you). Investment objectives are typically described in terms of one or more goals. These goals may include:

* Stability—protecting the principal (amount invested) from loss.

* Growth—increasing the value of the principal.

* Income—generating a constant flow of income through dividends.

The fund manager uses the investment objective as a guide when choosing investments for the fund's portfolio. Potential investors use it to determine which funds are suitable for their own needs. Mutual fund investment objectives cover a wide range. Some follow aggressive investment policies that involve greater risk in search of higher returns, others seek current income from more conservative investments.

Mutual funds, unlike bank deposits, are not insured or guaranteed by the Federal Deposit Insurance Corporation (FDIC) or any other government agency. Nor are they guaranteed by any bank or other financial institution—no matter how or where their shares are sold. Mutual funds involve investment risk, including the possible loss of principal. Of course, investment risk always includes potential for greater award as well.

When the fund earns money, it distributes the earnings to its shareholders. Money received by the fund as dividends from stocks held in its portfolio or as interest earned on its holdings of debt instruments (bonds) is paid out to fund shareholders as dividends. In addition, any earnings generated from securities sold for a profit are distributed to shareholders as capital gains. Dividends and distributions can be reinvested in the fund or received in cash. Dividends and capital gains produces are paid out in proportion to the number of shares owned. Thus, shareholders who invest a few hundred dollars get the same investment return per dollar as those who invest hundreds of thousands.

Investing in a mutual fund means buying shares of the fund. You would become an owner of shares in the fund just as you might own shares of stock in a large corporation. The difference is that a fund's only business is investing in many securities. A mutual fund does not manufacture anything or have a product, as an individual corporation would. The price of a mutual fund's shares is directly related to the value of the securities held by the fund. This collection of securities is known as the fund's portfolio.

Mutual funds continually issue new shares for purchase by the public. A fund's share price can change from day to day, depending on the daily value of the securities. The share price is called the net asset value (NAV) and is calculated very simply. The total value of the fund's investments at the end of the trading day (which is 4:00 p.m. eastern time), after expenses, is divided by the number of shares outstanding. Money market funds are typically managed to maintain a constant share price of $1.00.

Let me take just a moment to explain what a "Money Market" fund is. It's a market that's been created by the constant ebb and flow of people and organizations willing to lend and borrow money. These can be large companies or corporation's commercial paper (used by a corporation to finance short-term capital requirements). Usually this takes the form of notes with maturities from 1 to 270 days. Minimum amounts for these types of transactions are $50,000 but sometimes can go as low as $10,000. Overnight "purchase agreements," U.S. government agency discount notes, Federal agency obligations such as Federal National Mortgage Association (FNMA); Federal Home Loan Mortgage Corporation (FHLB); General National Mortgage Association (GNMA); Federal Home Loan Bank (FHLB) and some jumbo Certificate of Deposits would all fall into this category. A money market fund is generally known as one of the most conservative types of mutual funds.

WHO REGULATES MUTUAL FUNDS?

Mutual funds are highly regulated and must comply with some of the toughest laws and rules in the financial services industry. All funds are regulated by the U.S. Securities and Exchange Commission (SEC). The SEC, with its extensive rule making and enforcement authority, oversees mutual fund compliance with four major federal securities statutes.

The Securities Act of 1933 requires the fund's shares to be registered with the SEC prior to their sale. In essence, the Securities Act ensures that the fund provides potential investors with a current prospectus. The prospectus makes detailed disclosures about the fund's management, investment policies, objectives and investment activities. This law also limits the type of advertisements that may be used by a mutual fund. The Securities Exchange Act of 1934 regulates the purchase and sale of all types of securities, including mutual fund shares.

In addition to these federal statutes, almost every state has its own set of regulations governing mutual funds. While federal and state laws cannot guarantee that a fund will be profitable, they are designed to ensure that all mutual funds operate and conduct business in the interests of their shareholders. Here are some specific investor protections that every fund must follow:

* Regulations concerning what may be claimed or promised about a mutual fund and its potential.

* Requirements that vital information about a fund be made readily available such as a prospectus, the "statement of additional information"

(also known as part B of the registration statement), and the annual and semi-annual reports.

* Requirements that a fund operate in the interest of its shareholders, rather than any special interests of its management.

* Rules in the income tax laws dictating diversification of a fund's portfolio over a wide range of investments to avoid too much concentration in a particular security.

MUTUAL FUND INVESTMENT OBJECTIVES:

The Investment Company Institute classifies mutual funds into broad categories according to their basic investment objectives. They are:

Aggressive growth funds—seek maximum capital gains as their objective.

Balanced funds—generally have a three part investment objective.

1. to conserve investors' initial principal.

2. to pay current income.

3. to improve long-term growth of both principal and income.

Corporate bond funds—seek a high level of income by purchasing bonds of corporations.

Flexible portfolio funds—may be 100 percent invested in stocks or bonds or money market instruments.

Ginnie Mae Funds—seek high level of income by investing in mortgage securities backed by the Government National Mortgage Association (GNMA).

Global bond funds—seek a high level of income by investing in the debt securities of companies and countries worldwide, including the U.S.

Global equity funds—seek growth in the value of their investments in equity securities traded worldwide, including the U.S.

Growth funds—invest in the common stock of well-established companies.

Growth and income funds—invest mainly in the common stock of companies that have had increasing share value but also solid record of paying dividends.

High-yield bond funds—maintain at least two-thirds of their portfolios in lower-rated corporate bonds (Baa or lower by Moody's rating service and BBB or lower by Standard & Poor's).

Income-bond funds—seek a high level of current income by investing at all times in a mix of corporate and government bonds.

Income-equity funds—seek a high level of current income by investing primarily in equity securities of companies with good dividend-paying records.

Income-mixed funds—seek a high level of current income by investing in income-producing securities, including both equities and debt securities.

International funds—seek growth in value of their investments by investing in equity securities of companies outside the U.S. (two-thirds must be outside the U.S.).

National municipal bond funds—invest in bonds issued by states and municipalities to finance schools, highways, hospitals, airports, bridges, water and sewer works, and other public projects.

Precious metals/gold funds—seek an increase in the value of their investments by investing at least two-thirds of their portfolios in securities associated with gold, silver, and other precious metals.

Taxable money market mutual funds—seek to maintain a stable net asset value by investing in the short-term, high-grade securities sold in the money market.

Tax-exempt money market funds—seek tax-free investments with minimum risk.

U.S. Government income funds—seek current income by investing in a variety of government securities, including U.S. Treasury bonds, federally guaranteed mortgage-backed securities, and other government notes.

FIXED INCOME SECURITIES

15

Americans have more money invested in bonds than in stocks, mutual funds, or any other type of securities. One of the major appeals is that bonds pay a set amount of interest on a regular basis. That's why they are called fixed income securities. Another attraction is that the issuer promises to repay the loan in full and on time. So, bonds seem less risky than investments that depend on the ups and downs of the stock market.

Every bond has a fixed maturity date. The maturity date is when the bond expires and the loan must be paid back in full, at "par" value. The interest a bond pays is also set when the bond is issued. The rate is competitive, which means the bond pays interest comparable to what investors can earn elsewhere on other fixed income investments.

Investors can buy bonds issued by U.S. companies, by the U.S. Treasury, by various cities and states, and various federal, state and local government agencies. Many overseas companies and governments also sell bonds to U.S. investors. When those bonds are sold in U.S. dollars rather than the currency of the issuing country, they're sometimes known as "Yankee Bonds." There is an advantage for individual investors, in that they don't have to worry about currency fluctuations in figuring the bond's worth.

A LOOK AT THE WORLD OF BONDS

Type of Bond	Par Value	Maturity Period
Corporate Bonds	$1,000	1–5 years (short)
		5–10 years (mid)
		10–20 years (long)
Municipal Bonds	$5,000 and up	From 1 month to 40 years
Treasury Bonds and Treasury Notes	From $1,000 to $1 million	Bonds—over 10 yrs
		Notes—2 to 10 yrs
Treasury Bills	Usually $10,000 could be up to $1 million	3 & 6 months and 1 year
Agency Bonds	From $1,000 up to $25,000	From 30 days to 20 years

RATING BONDS

When you purchase a bond you want to be reasonably sure that you will get your interest payments on time principal back at maturity. It's almost impossible for an individual to do the necessary research. But there are rating services that make a business of this type of study.

The best-known services are Standard & Poor's, Moody's and Fitch. These companies carefully investigate the financial condition of a bond issuer rather than the market appeal of the bond. They look at other debt the issuer has, how fast the company's revenues and profits are growing, the state of the economy, and how well other companies in the same business (or municipal governments in the same general shape) are going. Their primary concern is to alert investors to risks of a particular issue.

Issuers rarely publicize their ratings, unless they are top of the line. So investors need to get the information from the rating services themselves, from the media, or from a qualified investment professional.

The information below shows how these three rating services grade bonds. The first four from each rating service are considered "Investment Grade" bonds, while the lower graded are considered "Junk" bonds. This means that there's a greater-than-average chance that the issuer will fail to repay the debt. The highly publicized mergers and takeovers of the 1980s were financed with junk bond issues. Corporations sold high risk bonds to the public. Investors were willing to take the risk because the yields were so much higher than other, safer bonds.

EXPLANATION OF CORPORATE/MUNICIPAL BOND RATINGS

	Rating with:		
Type	*Moody's*	*Standard & Poor's*	*Fitch*
(The first four are "Investment Grade")			
Highest Quality "Gift Edged"	Aaa	AAA	AAA
High Quality	Aa	AA	AA
Upper Medium Grade	A	A	A
Medium Grade	Baa	BBB	BBB
Predominantly Speculative	Ba	BB	BB
Speculative, Low Grade	B	B	B
Poor to Default	Caa	CCC	CCC
Highest speculation	Ca	CC	CC
Lowest Quality, No Interest	C	C	C
In various stage of default questionable value	Does not Rate these at all	DDD DD D	DDD DD D

Before investing in bonds, it's important to understand the factors that will affect your return and influence your direction. The credit quality measures that financial strength of the issuer to help you determine how capable it is of making interest payments and repaying the loan. This can be measured using the ratings from the chart on the previous page.

Maturity is the length of time the issuer has to return the money it borrowed. Ordinarily the longer the maturity, the higher the interest rate should be.

Liquidity means the access you have to your investments. You can sell most bonds anytime, then use the proceeds for other purposes. But when you sell a bond before maturity, you're selling at the current market price, which may be less than what you originally paid for it. Some bonds will have call features. Call features allow the issuer to buy back the bond before the date of maturity. When the bond is called, the issuer repurchases it at or above its face(or "par") value and stops paying interest on that loan.

THE RELATIONSHIP BETWEEN INTEREST RATES AND BOND PRICES

When interest rates move up or down, the price of the bond usually moves in the opposite direction. Short-term bonds are usually less affected by changes in interest rates than long-term bonds. The interest rate that the bond is paying does not actually change. If interest rates go down, then this bond will be paying more than the "current market" rates. This means that your bond is worth more to someone who needs higher income. In other words, you can charge more for your bond. Conversely, if interest rates go up, another investor could get a higher rate on the market. This means your bond will be worth less. Interest rates and bond prices fluctuate similar to a seesaw. When interest rates drop, the value of the existing bonds usually goes up. When rates climb, the value of existing bonds usually falls.

TAKING STOCK

16

What business has only three locations, has been doing business since 1792, and serves millions of customers daily from all over the world? The answer is the U.S. stock market where billions of dollars change hands every day! The stock market sells shares of stock representing ownership in various companies as well as hopes and dreams of wealth.

WHY DO WE HAVE A STOCK MARKET?

Say you started your business and it looks like it will be as successful as you had hoped. But to expand it you need MORE space, MORE computers, MORE supplies, MORE employees.... In other words, you need MORE money! It takes a lot of money to expand a business, you need investors, people who are willing to give you money in exchange for a piece of the action—a percentage of ownership.

One way to find investors is to hire an underwriter. This is generally a company, not a person and this company will help you go through the steps needed to sell a percentage of your company on one of the exchanges. The investors receive a piece of paper called a stock certificate that represents their percentage of ownership. Actually, in this day and age, most stock and bond trades are listed on the computer at your brokerage firm and you do not actually receive a piece of paper. But, I digress . . .

Buying stock in a company gives you the chance to share in the earnings of the company by way of dividends and capital appreciation. Dividends are a portion of the company's earnings distributed to the shareholders. Capital appreciation, on the other hand, is the increase in the value of the stock beyond what you paid for it.

WHERE IS THE EXCHANGE LOCATED?

The U.S. stock market is made up of several different stock exchanges. It includes the New York Stock Exchange (NYSE), the American Stock Exchange (AMEX) and the National Market System Automated Quotation (NASDAQ). The New York and American exchanges are in New York City and work like an auction. The NASDAQ, like the Internet, is a system of computers linked together. These stock exchanges make up the major portion of the U.S. stock market. The difference between the stock exchanges is found in the size of the companies they serve.

The NYSE is associated with having the most financially stable companies "listed" among its members. This is because it is the oldest exchange, started in 1792, and requires the members to have high net worth and earnings. It also has the highest listing fees, starting at around $50,000.

More mid-size companies can be found on the AMEX. The AMEX, founded in 1953, used to be called Curb Market Traders because the brokers used to trade on the sidewalk outside the NYSE. The listing or membership requirements of net worth and earnings are not as high as those found on the NYSE. Fees start at under $10,000.

The NASDAQ was organized in 1971. There is no trading floor for the NASDAQ as with the NYSE and AMEX. Instead, dealers input into the computer network the number of stock shares they have, at what price they would be willing to sell these shares and at what price they would be willing to buy shares. As the cheapest and easiest exchange to join, the NASDAQ is often thought of as representing small, start-up companies that have the potential to grow rapidly. Its technologically advanced system, though, is attracting larger companies. As a result, the NASDAQ is the fastest-growing of the three exchanges.

If your company has publicly traded stock but is not "listed" then it is part of the Over the Counter (O.T.C.) market. The O.T.C. publishes prices of "unlisted" stock. These companies do not qualify for membership in the NYSE, AMEX or NASDAQ.

SHARING A CORPORATION

Stocks are pieces of the corporate pie. When you buy stocks, you own a slice of the company. A corporation's stockholders, or shareholders (sometimes thousands of people) all have equity in the company, or own a fractional portion of the whole. You buy the stocks because you expect to profit when the company profits. Companies issue two types of stock: common and preferred.

Common stocks are ownership shares in a corporation. They are sold initially by the corporation and then traded among investors. Common stocks offer no performance guarantees, but over time have produced a better return than other investments. The risks you take when you buy stocks are that the individual company will not do well, or that stock prices will weaken. At worst, it's possible to lose an entire investment, though not more than that. Shareholders are not responsible for corporate debt.

Preferred stocks are also ownership shares issued by a corporation and traded by investors. They differ from common stocks in several ways, which reduce investor risk but also limit reward. The amount of the dividend is guaranteed and is paid before dividends on common stock. But the dividend isn't increased if the company profits, and the price of preferred stock increases more slowly. Preferred stockholders have a greater chance of getting some of their investment back if a company fails.

STOCK SPLITS

When the price of a stock gets too high, investors are often reluctant to buy, either because they think it has reached its peak or because it costs so much. Corporations have the option of splitting the stock to lower the price and stimulate trading. When a stock is split, there are more shares available but the total market value is the same. Say a company's stock is trading at $100 a share. If the company declares a two-for-one split, it gives every shareholder two shares for each one they held. At the same time the price drops to $50 a share. An investor who owned 300 shares at $100 now has 600 shares at $50—but the value is still $30,000. The initial effect is no different than getting change for a dollar. But there are more shares available, at a more accessible price. Stocks can split three-for-one, three-for-two, ten-for-one, or any combination. Stocks that have split within the last 52 weeks are identified in the *Wall Street Journal*'s stock columns with an $ in the left margin.

REVERSE SPLITS

In a reverse split you exchange more stocks for fewer (say two-for-five) and the price increases accordingly. Reverse splits are sometimes used to raise a stock's price. This discourages small investors who are costly to keep track of and may attract institutional investors who refuse to buy stock which costs less than their minimum requirement (often $5.00 a share).

Equity securities are designed for investors willing to accept some degree of market volatility in exchange for greater long-term growth potential. The amount of volatility can vary widely depending on the specific security. Preferred stocks or shares of utility companies tend to fluctuate less than emerging growth stocks.

In order to select securities that best meet your objectives, it is helpful to consider the beta of a specific stock or mutual fund.

Beta is a numerical rating assigned to a stock or mutual fund based on its volatility when compared with the Standard & Poor's 500 Index. A beta of 1.00 is assigned to the S&P 500. A beta of .65 indicates that a specific investment has been 35 percent less volatile than the S&P 500; a rating of 1.40, however, indicates it is 40 percent more volatile than the S&P 500. There must be at least three years of performance history before a security is assigned a beta rating.

FIVE MYTHS ABOUT ESTATE PLANNING

17

No matter what our ages or incomes, we all share a common goal to preserve for our family, friends, and charities the wealth we've worked so hard to earn. So why do only 30 percent of us have a will, according to the American Bar Association? Contrary to popular belief, estate planning isn't only for the privileged few and it doesn't have to be complicated.

MYTH #1
"I'M TOO YOUNG TO NEED A WILL."

Wills are not a question of age, but of circumstances. If you have a family, if you have responsibilities, if you have plans for your money after you're gone, you need a will to:

* Decide who raises your children. A will allows you to name the guardians who will care for your children.

* Distribute your wealth according to your wishes.

* Determine who will manage your estate. A will is the document in which you appoint an executor, the person responsible for paying your debts and carrying out your legacy. Passing away without a will (often referred to as "dying intestate") leaves these important decisions in the hands of a judge. If you don't have a will, the state in which you live decides how your

property will be passed on to your heirs. As you can imagine, the state's plans for your money can be very different from what you had in mind.

MYTH # 2

"I'M NOT RICH ENOUGH TO NEED A WILL."

Think of it this way: The less you have, the more you need to protect. Besides, your estate can grow surprisingly valuable after adding up your home, investment portfolio, life insurance, 401(k)s, IRAs, and personal property such as cars, jewelry, and art.

MYTH #3

"I HAVE A WILL, SO MY ESTATE PLAN IS COMPLETE."

Even where there's a will, there may be a better way. While wills can be important estate planning tools, they do have drawbacks:

* Wills are validated in probate court, which can be a costly and time-consuming process that makes your affairs part of the public record.

* Children take control of assets bequeathed to them at the age of majority (Usually 18 or 21, check with your state) which is often too young to manage the responsibilities of an inheritance.

* If you die, your children's guardian may be requested to submit to a probate judge an annual budget and investment strategy, which can't be changed without court approval. State laws require these steps to guard against mismanagement, but it puts a heavy burden on the caretaker.

A TRUST CAN HELP

You can sidestep these pitfalls with a trust, which is simply a legal document allowing you to spell out how and when you wish to distribute your estate. You also name the trustee (this could be a friend, relative, professional trust manager, or investment management firm) who will manage your trust. There are many varieties of trust, but only two basic types:

1. A *testamentary trust* is created as part of your will and moves your designated assets into a trust upon death.

2. An *inter vivos trust* is created outside your will (often as a revocable "living trust" or "loving trust"). Although your assets are in a trust, you continue to control them by acting as the trustee. Then, after your death, a successor trustee manages your legacy on your heir's behalf. Testamentary trusts, like wills, pass through probate court, while inter vivos trust do not.

MYTH #4
"ESTATE PLANNING IS TOO EXPENSIVE."

Not really. According to the National Resource Center for Consumers of Legal Services, the legal costs for a simple will are just $75. The fees for most common trusts usually range from $500 to $1,500. This may seem like a great deal of difference. But contrast those low costs with the high price of probate, which the National Association of Financial and Estate Planning estimate at 6 to 10% of an estate's value. The fees for a court-appointed executor generally take up another three to five percent of your estate if you don't have a will.

MYTH # 5
"THE MAIN GOAL OF ESTATE PLANNING IS TO CUT TAXES."

It's true that federal estate taxes can be, well, taxing (starting at 37% and escalating to 60%). Only 2% of estates, however, are taxed. Why? Because the first $625,000 of an estate is exempt from federal taxes. Any assets over this amount , which gradually rises to $1 million by the year 2006, are taxable. The table may be helpful:

YEAR	EXCLUSION
1998	$ 625,000
1999	$ 650,000
2000	$ 675,000
2001	$ 675,000
2002	$ 700,000

2003	$ 700,000
2004	$ 850,000
2005	$ 950,000
2006	$1,000,000

A married person can leave a tax-free inheritance of any size to a spouse who's a U.S. citizen. And any person can reduce their estate by giving tax-free gifts of up to $10,000 per person, per year.

CONSIDER THESE ESTATE PLANNING TIPS:

* *Review your estate plan every three to five years. Changes in your marital status, home address, or family situation may signal the need to redraft your will and trusts.*

* *Pay the medical and education bills for relatives and friends. No matter what the amount, these gifts are tax-free as long as payments are made directly to the school or medical provider.*

* *Some trusts must be made irrevocable, which means that the terms of the trust can never be changed. Be sure to fully consider the implications of your decision to commit assets to an irrevocable trust (or any trust, for that matter). Consult with your attorney or advisor for guidance.*

The tax laws governing estate are complicated and always changing. It's a good idea to consult with your attorney and financial advisor to discuss your future plans. A little planning today can help to improve the quality of life for your heirs tomorrow.

PROPERTY RIGHTS AND WAYS TO TAKE TITLE

18

There are many legal distinctions among the various types of property. These distinctions govern how property is treated. United States law is heavily derived from English legal principals, except for intellectual property law, whose major developments arose after the United States had become a separate political entity. Intellectual property law is governed primarily by the interaction of Federal and state statutes. Intellectual property issues arose much later than the issues of real and personal property.

I hope you find the following distinctions useful:

A. Personal property (includes tangible, movable things) as a definition originally referred to those items of property for which a "personal action" could be brought in feudal times. Today, tangible personal property includes vehicles, furniture, pictures, carpets, dishes, equipment, livestock, clothing, jewelry, and other such movable things not permanently affixed to real property.

Intangible personal property includes that which has physical properties but that primarily is representative—such as stocks, bonds, accounts receivable, contracts, leases, franchises, licenses, options, bank and financial accounts.

B. Real Property

Originally, this meant that kind of property for which a "real action" could be brought in feudal times. It usually is land and things permanently on or in the land (buildings, walls, trees, etc.). Examples of real property are: a mine; trees; built-ins, such as cabinets, lighting fixtures, or plumbing pipes. Some things may be either real or personal, depending upon the agreement between buyer and seller, such as ripe fruit. The status of any uncertain property should be described in the written purchase agreement for real property.

Some things that may appear to be part of the real property can be severed and treated separately, such as rights of way, mineral rights, timber, or crops. When in doubt, ask the attorney who is drawing up the contract to spell out specifically the terms pertaining to items that you have questions about.

INTELLECTUAL PROPERTY

Generally, this deals with intangible property rights in three legal rears: copyrights, patents, and trademarks, under which fall things such as trade secrets, unfair competition, authors' rights, licensings, and technology transfer. Intellectual property law is especially intricate and highly specialized. Stakes involved can sometimes be very high.

Legally, then, the three categories of property law with distinct bodies of statues, regulations, and case law are real, personal and intellectual. In general, real property usually has to do with real estate; personal property usually is something tangible or a claim on something tangible; and intellectual property deals with the right to use creative ideas or works.

WHO MAY TRANSFER PROPERTY?

Anyone of legal age and sound mind who has not been legally restrained may transfer property legally belonging to them. A guardian may apply to the court of jurisdiction for approval to transfer the property of a minor or incompetent person. State statutes, regulations, and case law, and an attorney should be consulted about complex personal situations.

OWNERSHIP OF PROPERTY

Our system of property ownership generally is based on English legal habits brought to America. Ownership of personal property usually is established by holding the item itself and the title to that item. For example, an item of jewelry or furniture when paid for, or once an agreement is made to pay, is handed over to the purchaser and a receipt is given. The purchaser leaves the store with both the item in possession and the indication of where title resides, in hand.

Real property ownership is more complex, in part because ownership of real property by private individuals arose relatively late in England. A fundamental rule of real property ownership, one that cannot be contravened, has to do with "alienation." Alienation refers to the ability to keep property in use. Real property ownership laws are structured to favor those who claim and use property rather than those who merely hold property. Thus, for example, trying to keep property "in the family" for several generations, by preventing the kind of full ownership that allows the owner to do with the property what he or she wants, can result in a court declaration of full title to one family member, who will then be able to use the property (or sell it), rather than allow it to lie fallow because of title constraints.

If the owner of record neglects real property to the extent of not realizing someone else has laid claim to the land and has been using it for a period of years (set by the state), title will pass to the person using it rather than remain with the owner of record if the user/claimant meets all the criteria set by the state for "adverse possession." A patriarch who wants to keep the family property in the family for perpetuity may find his or her bequest settled "in fee simple" upon the first or possibly second holder of the property under the will, regardless of a wish that the property be held.

THE IMPORTANCE OF "HOW" YOU HOLD TITLE

If there is only one owner, that person owns the property in fee simple. But if there is more than one owner, the language setting up the form of ownership is significant. If this language is not clear, unintended consequences may cause both legal and financial hardship. The commonly used forms of plural ownership are: tenancy in common, joint tenancy, and tenancy by the entirety.

Tenancy in common is the form of ownership in which two or more parties own the property in question, but each owns a separate piece of the property rights. A tenant in common may separately dispose of that property interest in any legal way, to any person, without directly affecting the ownership rights of any of the other tenants in common.

JOINT TENANCY

Joint tenancy is a form of ownership where several parties each own the whole of the property in question, owing to four unities that must be observed at inception in order to create a joint tenancy.

There must be:

1. A single property interest that is created by the same instrument as to all of the owners.

2. A single property interest that is identical as to each of the owners.

3. Each must begin owning at the same time.

4. Each must own the property by one and the same undivided possession.

TENANCY BY THE ENTIRETY

This form of ownership is possible only between husband and wife, where each owns the whole of the property. This form of tenancy observes all of the unities present in joint tenancy and also must be legal.

CONCLUSION

It is my belief that every woman needs and deserves some fundamental information concerning investments. It is my intent, through this book, to help you to gain a beginning level of knowledge and understanding of budgeting and cash flow, risk management and investments. For women, there seems to be a mystery about investing. I hope to have removed some of that mystery for you.

The number of possible investment alternatives is virtually unlimited. Please continue to research and learn about your investment choices. Find a qualified investment professional to help you and ask many questions. This book should be viewed for what it is . . . a start on your journey to future financial success.

RESOURCES CONSULTED

American Association for Retired Persons, Publication 100542, 1997

American Association of University Women

American Institute for Economic Research, Great Barrington, Massachusetts

Brown, Eryn; Carvell, Tim, "Women Sex & Power," *Fortune* magazine, Aug. 5, 1996

Creswell, Julie, "Is Your Future Left to Chance?," *Money* magazine, July 1996

Internal Revenue Service

International Association for Financial Planning

Journal of Population Economics, February 1994; August 1995; March 1997; December 1997; April–August 1998

Korn/Ferry International, *Decade of Executive Women*, 1998

Merrill Lynch, Financial Survey, 1993

National Association of Investors Corporation

National Center for Education Statistics

National Center for Women and Retirement Research

National Council of State Housing Agencies

National Foundation for Consumer Credit, *No Quick Fixes*, September 1997

National Survey of Statistics, 1997

New York Life Insurance Company, Gallup Poll, 1997

Social Security Administration, *Understanding the Benefits*, June 1997

U.S. Census Bureau

U.S. Department of Labor, *The Glass Ceiling Commission Mission Statement*, 1993

U.S. Department of Labor, *Pipelines of Progress: A Status Report on the Glass Ceiling*, 1992

Van Kampen, *Your Portfolio*, August 1998

Working Woman magazine (including the Executive Female Section for the National Association for Female Executives—NAFE)

ABOUT THE AUTHOR

Diane K. Keister is a Certified Financial Planner and Chartered Financial Consultant. She has completed her Series 7 (General Securities Representatives), 63 (Uniform Securities Agent), and 65 (Uniform Investment Advisor Law Examination). These licenses are designed to test the knowledge of state and federal securities laws and regulations applicable to those giving investment advise. She also holds Life, Accident, and Health Insurance licenses. Diane holds a Bachelor Degree in Business and is currently completing her Master's Degree in Financial Services (MSFS). She has over 14 years experience in various aspects of the financial arena.

Diane has recently been nominated to be listed in the Kensington Who's Who, The International Who's Who of Professionals.

Conducting seminars, discussions groups, and individual coaching is just part of what Diane does for women and women's groups. She has been involved in Girl Scouting for over 25 years and was a leader for eight years. She also was a volunteer for the American Red Cross for ten years and on one of their Boards of Directors for nine years.

Writing several columns for various magazines and newspapers is just another example of how Diane tries to share the "Women and Investing" message with women from all walks of life. Diane has a forward thinking style that is exceptional. She is a person who motivates others, guides them, and encourages them. She is an inspiration to businesswomen and all women!

GLOSSARY

Accept—The taking of a risk (by an underwriter or another person authorized to act) by expressing a willingness to issue insurance.

Accidental bodily injury—If the result of an action results in an accidental injury a policy written on an accidental injury basis would cover the accident.

Accidental death—Refers to death from other than natural causes.

Accidental death plan—A benefit in addition to the face amount of a life insurance policy, payable if the insured dies as a result of an accident. Sometimes referred to as "double indemnity."

Accidental means—Both the result and the cause must be accidental.

Accumulation plan—A plan for the systematic accumulation of mutual fund shares through periodic investments and reinvestments of income dividends and capital gains distribution.

Accumulation stage—This is the period of time where the principal remains on deposit to accumulate interest on a tax-deferred basis.

Actively managed—Portfolios for total return bond strategy should be left to the desecration of a professional manager. When a market starts to fluctuate, adjustments are made.

Actuary—A person professionally trained in the technical aspects of insurance and related fields, particularly in the mathematics of insurance—such as the calculation of premiums, reserves and other values.

Additional insured—A person, other than the name insured, who is protected by the terms of the policy. Usually a specified individual such as a spouse or a member of the insured's family.

Adjustable life insurance—A type of insurance that allows the policyholder to change the plan of insurance, raise or lower the face amount of the policy, increase or decrease the premium and lengthen or shorten the protection period.

Adjustable rate preferred stock—A preferred stock whose dividends are adjusted to reflect market rates of interest, thereby eliminating interest rate risk.

Admitted company—A insurance company that is licensed to business in the state. The license is granted buy the insurance department of the state.

Adviser—The organization employed by a mutual fund to give professional advice on the fund's investment and asset management practices (also called the "investment adviser").

Agent—The common term that applies to a person who sells insurance. The agent has powers to represent the insurance company in the sale of and in the make up in the insurance contract

Agent—One who has authority to act for another.

Aggressive stock—Stocks that have Beta coefficients greater than one.

Alien company—An insurance company that is organized outside of the United States. A Canadian life insurance company would be an example of an alien company.

A.M. best rating—A. M. Best is the most widely recognized independent rating service in the insurance industry. Best rates the financial strength and operating performance of an insurance company in comparison to the norms of the life/health insurance industry. The Best rating does not refer to the quality of a specific product line.

American Depository Receipts (ADRs)—Certificates that represent ownership of foreign shares that are held abroad by United States banks located in a foreign country. They are subject to currency fluctuations and can be either growth or cyclical. The investor in an ADR receives both the dividend and the capital appreciation in U. S. dollars.

Amount of insurance—A limit of payment a company can be liable for under a policy.

Annualization—The term which applies to the provision whereby a policy issued for a period of more than one year is subject to the payment of annual premiums, often with the provision that the annual payment is made at the premium rate prevailing at the anniversary date. Note: May also apply to commission paid to an agent; *i.e.* if premiums are paid via monthly payment mode, the carrier may elect to annualize commissions and pay in advance to the agent, with the understanding that if the policy is canceled or payments lapse, the agent refunds these monies paid in advance.

Annual renewable agreement—Certain Policy forms contain a clause, whereby the company agrees to renew the policy for a certain number of times at some specified rate.

Annual and semiannual reports—Reports that a mutual fund sends to it's shareholders, which discuss the funds performance over the past period and identify the securities currently in the fund's portfolio.

Annual report—The formal financial statement issued yearly by a corporation to its shareholders. This report shows assets, liabilities, earnings, shareholders' equity, how the company stood at the end of the business year, and how it performed profit-wise during the year. It usually contains a separate signed report by the president and a letter attesting to the examination by the auditors.

Annuity—An annuity is a contract which provides for a systematic liquidation of the principal sum over a fixed period of time or over someone's life-time. Much like the amortization of a loan, the payments will be made up of both principal and interest.

Annuity—The payment of a sum of money, usually monthly, to a person for their lifetime. Often contains some form of refund feature or promise to pay for a certain length of time should the annuitant die before receiving a set sum or number of payments.

Annuitant—The annuitant is the individual whose life is being used to determine the characteristics of the payout phrase of the contract. In most cases, the annuitant and the owner are the same person.

Annuitant—The person who receives the annuity payment.

Annuitization—When the owner elects to annuitize a contract, he will be offered a choice of several payout options. These may include:

Annuitization stage—This is when the owner of the contract elects to apply the accumulated value of the contract towards a settlement option. This option can be for a stated period of time or for the life of the annuitant.

Application—A written statement by a prospective policyholder which gives the information the company relies upon when issuing the insurance.

Application—The instrument that is completed by the agent for the insurance company. The insurance company will make their decision to accept the risk based on the application and other supporting information. The application will become part of the life and health policy. Sometimes part of the application is completed by a medical person.

Appreciation—An increase in an investment's value.

A Shares—Front-end loads on mutual funds. With this type of sales load you pay the cost up front. You should stay in this type of fund for six years or longer.

Asked price—The price asked for a security offered for sale. Quoted, bid, and asking prices are wholesale prices for interdealers trading and do not represent prices for the public.

Ask (asked) price—The price at which the market maker is willing to sell a security to a buyer.

"Asked" or "offering price"—The price at which a mutual fund's shares can be purchased. The asked or offering price means the current net asset value per share plus sales charge, if any.

Assets—The investment holdings and cash owned by a mutual fund.

Asset allocation—Dividing investment funds among different types of investment assets.

Asset allocation manager—Makes bold portfolio movements. They can be one hundred percent invested in stock or one hundred percent in cash if they feel the market is vulnerable. Considered to be for more conservative investors, these managers will attempt to go to cash in a down market so you will not lose your money, however in an up market they will make less.

Asset plays—Involve undervalued assets on the books of a corporation. The idea is to take advantage of these undervalued items and buy low. This is an example of value investing.

Asset protection—The United States has 7% of the world's population and 70% of the world's attorneys. Protecting your assets from lawsuits is more important than ever. Furthermore, they will explain techniques that may help you achieve asset protection in the event of bankruptcy or property loss.

Assignee—The individual or other organization which receives the legal rights or interest in an insurance policy through an assignment.

Assignment—The transfer of the owner's rights in an insurance policy to another. Almost all life and health policies allow the assignment without the consent of the insurance company. The insurance company will not be bound by any assignment until it is received by the company. The word is also used to refer to the assignment of benefit payment under a policy to some third person or organization, such as hospital.

Assume—To accept (by an underwriter or another person authorized to act) all or part of a risk or an exposure, at which time insurance "attaches."

Authorization—A statement, written or oral, made by an underwriter to a producer, expressing the underwriter's ability, willingness and readiness to insure a certain risk, for a certain amount, on certain terms.

Automatic reinvestment—A shareholder-authorized purchase of additional shares using dividends and capital gains distribution.

Averages—Various ways of measuring the trend of stocks listed on exchanges. Formulas, some vary absolute, have been devised to compensate for stock splits and stock dividends and thus give continuity to the average. In case of the Dow-Jones Industrial Average, the prices of the thirty stocks are totaled and then divided by a figure that is intended to compensate for past stock splits and stock dividends and that is changed from time to time.

B

Bailout provision—Many fixed annuity contracts will have a bailout provision or a "keep 'em honest" clause. This clause states that if the insurance company declares a renewal rate that is lower than the initial guaranteed rate, all surrender charges will be waived and the client can move his money to another contract or another company without incurring penalties. This clause creates incentives for the insurance company to keep their renewal interest rates competitive.

Balanced fund—Fund that buys common stock, preferred stock and bonds in an effort to obtain the highest retrun consistent with a low-risk strategy.

Balanced managers—Manage stocks and bonds in the same portfolio.

Bear market—A securities market characterized by declining stock prices.

Benefits—In life, health and accident insurance, the money payable or service rendered under a policy.

Beneficiary—The person or entity named in a life insurance policy to receive the proceeds at the death of the insured.

Beneficiary—The person who is designated in the policy to receive the insurance proceeds upon the death of the insured. Unless named irrevocable the beneficiary can be changed at any time by the owner.

Beta coefficient—A measure of the systematic risk of a stock relative to the rest of the market.

Bid price—The highest price at which a market maker is willing to purchase a stock from a seller.

Bid or sell price—The price at which a mutual fund's shares are redeemed (bought back) by the fund. The bid or redemption price usually means the current net asset value per share.

Bid and asked—Often referred to as a quotation or quote. The bid is the highest price anyone has declared that he or she wants to pay for a security at a given time; the asked is the lowest price at which anyone will sell at the same time.

Big board—A popular term for the New York Stock Exchange, Inc.

Binder—An oral or written agreement to insure, which serves as evidence of the coverage prior to the issuance of a policy.

Binding receipt—A receipt that is given when an applicant is taken and first premium paid that actually provides interim insurance coverage until the company accepts or declines the insurance applied for.

Blue-chip stock—The common stock of a large, well-established corporation that has a history of steady earnings and paying regular dividends.

Blue sky laws—A popular name for the laws enacted by various states to protect the public against securities frauds. The term is believed to have originated when a judge ruled that a popular stock had about the same value as a patch of blue sky.

Bond—Basically an IOU or promissory note of a corporation, usually issued in multiples of $1000. A bond is evidence of a debt on which the issuing company usually promises to pay the bondholders a specified amount of interest for a specified length of time, and to repay the loan on the expiration date. In every case, a bond represents debt—its holder is a creditor of the corporation and not a part owner, as is the shareholder.

Bond fund—A mutual fund invested primarily in bonds.

Book value—The net worth of a company (total assets minus the total liabilities).

Book value—The assumed valuation of a company if it were liquidated—all assets minus all liabilities, divided by the number of shares outstanding.

Breakout—When the price of a stock rises significantly above a resistance level or declines significantly below a support level.

Broker—An agent who handles the public's order to buy and sell securities, commodities, or other property. A commission is usually charged for the service.

Bull market—A securities market characterized by increasing stock prices.

B shares—Are back-end loads on mutual funds. When using this structure, you pay deferred load when you sell the fund. It is a declining back-end load, which means the longer you hold the fund, the less of a sales load you will have to pay. Twelve B-1 fees are charged annually on back-end load funds.

Business cycle—A swing in economic activity over a period of time.

Business life insurance—A term that is applied to life insurance that is written to meet the various needs of a business. The use of life insurance provide funds for buy and sell agreements in a major use.

Business life insurance—Life insurance purchased by a business enterprise on the life of a member of the firm. It is often bought by partnerships to protect the surviving partners against loss caused by the death of a partner, or by the corporation to reimburse it for loss caused by the death of a key employee.

Business risk—The risk associated with the nature of the company's business.

Buy list—A list of company stock selected by DLJ that are expected to outperform the S&P 500 Index by at least 15% within the next 12 months.

Buy-and-sell agreements—This refers to the agreement that commits the surviving partners or stockholders (could also be the corporation itself) to purchase, and the survivors to sell the interest of the deceased partner or stockholder.

C

Callable—A bond issue, all or part of which may be redeemed by the issuing corporation under definite conditions before maturity. The term also applies to preferred shares, which may be redeemed by the issuing corporation.

Cancel—To terminate a contract. Usually applied to the termination of a policy before its natural expiration, but may be used to describe the ending of any contract during its natural life, such as an agent's contract.

Capitalization—The price of the stock times the amount of shares outstanding.

Capital growth—An increase in market value of a mutual fund's securities, as reflected in the net asset value of fund shares. This is a specific long-term objective of many mutual funds.

Capital stock—All shares representing ownership of a business, including preferred and common.

Capital gains distribution—Payments to mutual fund shareholders of profits (long-term gains) realized on the sale of the fund's portfolio securities. These amounts are usually paid once a year.

Capital gain or capital loss—Profit or loss from the sale of a capital asset. A capital gain, under current federal income tax laws, may be either short-term (6 months or less) or long-term (more than 6 months). A short-term capital gain is taxed at the reporting individual's full income tax rate. A long-term capital gain is taxed at the reporting individual's income tax rate with a maximum rate of 28%.

Carrier—The insurance company which provides the protection for a particular risk.

Cash surrender value—The amount available, in cash, upon voluntary termination of a policy by its owner before it becomes payable by death or maturity.

Cash surrender value—One of the nonforfeiture values. After a certain length of time permanent life insurance develops a cash value. The cash value is available to the insured when the policy lapses. It is necessary for the insured to elect this option upon the lapse of the policy.

Cash value—The cash value of an annuity contract is the accumulated value of the contract (principal plus earnings).

Certificate of insurance—A short-form documentation of an insurance policy.

Certificate—The piece of paper that is evidence of ownership of stock in a corporation. Loss of a certificate may cause, at least, a great deal of inconvenience; at worst, financial loss.

Claim—An amount requested of an insurer, by a policyholder or a claimant, for an insured loss.

Clause—Language in a policy which describes, limits or modifies coverage granted.

Close—The last price that a security trades at during the trading session.

Closed-end—Mutual fund shares are issued just one time, and are then traded on a major exchange like the New York Stock Exchange, just like an individual stock.

Closed-end mutual fund—An investment company that issues a fixed number of shares and does not redeem them. It may also issue senior securities and/or warrants.

Collateral—Securities or other property pledged by a borrower to secure repayment of a loan.

Commissions—The portion of the premium paid to the agent or broker for having produced the business.

Common stock—Securities that represent an ownership interest in a corporation. If the company has also issued preferred stock, both common and preferred have ownership rights. Claims of both common and preferred stockholders are junior claims of bondholders or other creditors of the company. Common stockholders assume greater risk but generally exercise greater control and may gain greater reward in the form of dividends and capital appreciation.

Common stock equivalent—Options, rights and warrants that can be used to purchase the underlying common stock of a company.

Common stock fund—A mutual fund that has a stated policy of investing most of its assets in common stocks. The term is also applied to funds that normally invest only in common stocks, though are not restricted to do so by charter.

Commodities Research Bureau Index—(CRB Index) A composite of commodities like the Dow Jones Industrial Average is a composite for stocks.

Compounding—Earnings on your investment's earnings. For example, if you invested $1000 earnings of 5% a year, after one year, you would have $1,050. During the second year, you will earn interest not only on the original $1000, but also on the $50 in earnings. Over time, compounding can lead to significant growth in your investment.

Comprehensive medical expense policy—A policy that combines in one contract the first dollar coverage of basic insurance plan and the high limits of the major medical policy. The comprehensive medical expense policy is found in group insurance.

Commissioner of insurance—The official of a state charged with the duty of enforcing its insurance laws. Also called the superintendent of insurance (3 states) and director of insurance (8 states). The official is elected in 11 states, appointed by a governor or state agency in 38 states, and a civil service appointee in Colorado.

Concealment—In insurance, failure to disclose a material fact which may void an insurance policy.

Condition—Something established or agreed upon to be necessary to make a policy of insurance effective.

Conditional receipt—The generally used conditional receipt will make the insurance effective upon the date of the receipt if the applicant for insurance is found to meet the insurance company's selection criteria (underwriting standards).

Confirmation—A written description of the terms of a securities transaction, supplied by broker/dealer to their customers or to other broker/dealers.

Consideration—An essential element of a contract. To be enforceable, contract must contain the essential elements, one of which is consideration. It is what each party gives in return for the consideration of the other party. The insured gives a premium an application. The company gives a promise to pay.

Constructive receipts—A doctrine of the IRS that requires the reporting of income (including capital gains) in the year in which it could have been received had a taxpayer so wished. Thus, dividends of a mutual fund automatically reinvested are taxable in the year reinvested on the basis that the taxpayer could have received them in cash at his or her option.

Constant dollar plan—A formula for investing in which the investor maintains a fixed dollar amount in the portion of the portfolio allocated to stocks or bonds. This requires buying or selling securities to maintain the fixed dollar amount of a periodic basis.

Constant ratio plan—A formula plan for investing whereby the investor maintains a fixed ratio among the types of securities in the portfolio. This requires buying or selling different types of securities to restore the constant ratio of the assets within the portfolio.

Contingent beneficiary—It is customary to name another beneficiary to receive the insurance proceeds should the primary beneficiary die prior to the insured.

Contingent Deferred Sales Charge—(CDSC) A fee imposed when shares are redeemed (sold back to the fund) during the first few years of share ownership.

Contract execution—When does the policy take effect? Except as provided in the conditional receipt, the policy is effective when it is issued, delivered and premium paid.

Contract owner—The owner of an annuity contract is the individual who controls the cash value in the accumulation stage. The owner has the right to allow the cash value to remain on deposit, take a cash withdrawal, move the money to another contract, elect to annuitize the contract, or change the beneficiary. The contract owner receives the monthly payments upon annuitization of the contract.

Conversion privilege—A provision in a group policy that allows the insured member of the group to convert to an individual life or accident and health policy without evidence of insurability upon his or her leaving the group. The insured has 31 days in which to exercise the conversion.

Convertible—A bond, debenture, or preferred share that may be exchanged by the owner for common stock or another security, usually of the same company, in accordance with the terms of the issue.

Convertible preferred stock—A preferred stock that may at the holder's option be converted into a fixed number of common shares of that company.

Convertible term—A contractual right under the term life insurance policy to convert the term insurance to some form of permanent life insurance.

Convertible term insurance—Term Insurance which can be exchanged, at the option of the policy holder and without evidence of insurability, for another plan of insurance.

Corporate bond—An evidence of indebtedness issued by a corporation, rather than the U.S. Government or municipality.

Correction—A correction is a decline in market indexes over a rather short period of time which ranges from a few days to a few weeks, but no longer than 2 to 3 months. The price decline usually on the order of 5 to 15%.

Coupon bond—Bond with interest coupons attached. The coupons are clipped as they come due and are presented by the holder for payment of interest.

Cover—1) To protect with insurance; 2) the insurance itself. Same as coverage.

Coverage—The extent of insurance protection afforded by a policy of insurance.

Crash—A crash is a sudden, severe decline in prices (as we saw on Oct. 19, 1987) which lasts only a day or two and results in declines of major market averages of 15% or more.

Credit life or accident and health—Insurance, usually written under a group plan, that will pay off the loan upon the death of the borrower. The creditor is the beneficiary. The accident and health policy will make the loan payments to the creditor if the insured becomes disabled.

Credit insurance—A form of life and health insurance protecting the lender against loss from death or disability of the borrower, often written as group insurance. The coverage can be written to protect the interest of the creditor only (single interest), or the interests of the creditor or debtor.

Credit risk—Financial and moral risk that an obligation will not be paid and a loss will result.

Cum-rights—The period during which the preemptive rights accompany the purchase or sale of the underlying common stock.

Cumulative preferred—A preferred stock for which unpaid dividends accumulate in arrears and must be paid before any common dividends are paid.

Cumulative voting—A method of voting for corporate directors that allows shareholders to place their votes in any combination they choose.

Cut-through endorsement—An addition to an insurance policy between an insurance company and a policyholder which requires that, in the event of the company's insolvency, any part of a loss covered by reinsurance be paid directly to the policyholder by the reinsurer.

Current assets—Those assets of a company that are reasonably expected to be realized in cash, or sold or consumed during the normal operating cycle of the business.

Current asset—An asset that will be converted into cash within one year.

Current liability—An obligation that will be paid within one year.

Current ratio—A measure of a company's liquidity. The ability to pay off its current obligations from the turnover of its current assets into cash.

Custodian—The organization (usually a bank) that keeps custody of securities and other assets of a mutual fund.

C Shares—Mutual funds that have no front-end loads, but they do have a higher management fee. If you plan to hold the fund for five years or more, a front-ended load may be better.

CSO—This refers to the Commissioners Standard Ordinary table which gives both the probability of dying and of surviving at particular age. It is often simply called the mortality table.

Cyclical stocks—Are sensitive to economic cycles. The earnings per share can be based on the strength or weakness in the economy. Cyclical stocks may pay higher quarterly dividends to the stockholders instead of reinvesting the profits into the company. There are three types of cyclical stocks: large-cap, mid-cap, and small-cap.

Cyclical industry—An industry whose financial health is tied to the economy.

D

Date of record—The date on which the shareholders must be registered owners of the shares in order to receive the dividends.

Day order—An order that is canceled if it is not executed on the day it was entered.

Debit-to-equity ratio—The ratio of total debt to total equity

Debit or loaner investments—Investments where you loan your money to someone else, either the U.S. government, a corporation, or a city, and you are paid interest for the use or, in other words, the issuer will raise taxes without limit to repay you.

Declaration—A statement made to the company or to its agents by a policy-holder, upon which the company may rely in undertaking the insurance.

Declaration date—The date on which the board of directors announces the amount and date of the next dividend, rights offering or stock split.

Declared interest rate—The interest rate the insurance company is currently paying on new deposits. This interest rate is typically guaranteed for one year.

Declination—The rejection by a life insurance company of an application for life insurance, usually for reasons of the health or occupation of the applicant.

Decreasing term—A form of term life insurance where the face amount of insurance decreases with the passage of time. It is used to provide protection for temporary needs that become smaller as the months and years go by.

Defensive stock—Stocks whose prices remain stable or go up when the general economy is in recession. These stocks have beta coefficients of less than one. Examples are food, soap and utility stocks. These are companies that make products people need, even in a recession.

Deferred premium payment plan—Provides for the payment of premium in installments. An initial installment is due upon attachment of liability with additional installments payable at monthly, bi-monthly, or quarterly periods.

Dental care—A relatively new group insurance benefit that pays the covered members for dental care. It is usually subject to a deductible and/or percentage participation on the part of the insured group member.

Depletion—Natural resources such as metals, oils, gases and timber that conceivably can be reduced to zero over the years present a special problem in capital management. Depletion is an accounting practice consisting of charges against earnings based upon the amount of the asset taken out of the total reserves in the period for which accounting is made. A bookkeeping entry, it does not represent any cash outlay, nor are any funds earmarked for the purpose.

Deposit premium—A tentative charge made at the beginning of certain policies, to be adjusted when the actual earned charge has been later determined. Also known as Initial Premium.

Deposit term insurance—A form of the term insurance in which the first-year premium is larger than subsequent premiums. Typically, a partial endowment is paid at the end of the term period. In many cases the partial endowment can be applied toward the purchase of a new term policy or, perhaps, a whole life policy.

Depreciation—A decline in an investment's value.

Disability benefits—A feature added to some life insurance policies providing for wavier of premium, and sometimes payment of monthly income, if the policyholder becomes partially and/or totally and permanently disabled.

Disability and death protection—Inadequate income replacement protection can wipe out a financial portfolio with amazing speed. Your future goals should be achieved regardless of your ability to consistently go to work. Similarly, your death could leave your family in a terrible financial mess. A good plan guarantees that the people you love can always count on you—even if you should become disabled or die.

Discount rate—The rate the federal reserve charges banks to borrow money.

Dismemberment—A coverage found in accident and health policies that pay a lump sum when the insured suffers a loss of limb(s) or sight. The policy may or may not require actual severance of the limb. The more liberal policy requires simply loss of use.

Distribution—1) The payment of dividends and capital gains. 2) A term used to describe a method of sales.

Diversification—The policy of all mutual funds to spread investments among a number of different securities to reduce the risk inherent in investing.

Diversification—Spreading investments among different companies in different fields. Another type of diversification is offered by the securities of many individual companies because of the wide range of their activities.

Diversification—A portfolio of different securities in different industries to minimize the risk of loss.

Dividend—That part of the premium that is returned to the insured (in cash, as paid up additions or left to accumulate at interest) under a participating policy. This return is the result of better investment earnings, lower expenses and decreased mortality.

Dividend—The payment designated by the board of directors to be distributed prorate among the shares outstanding. Preferred shares generally pay a fixed dividend, while common shares pays a dividend that varies with the earnings of the company and the amount of cash on hand. Dividends may be omitted if business is poor or the directors withhold earnings to invest in plant and equipment. Sometimes a company will pay a dividend out of post earnings even if it is not currently operating at a profit.

Dividend reinvestment plan—A mutual fund share account in which dividends are automatically reinvested in additional shares. With this type of account, capital gains distributions are also automatically reinvested. Dividends (but not capital gains) may be reinvested at offering price (*i.e.*, with a sales charge), but more commonly reinvested at the asset value.

Dividend reinvestment plan—A plan in which shareholders elect to have the company reinvest their cash dividends to purchase additional shares of stock of the company.

Dollar-cost averaging—The practice of investing equal amounts of money at regular intervals regardless of whether securities markets are moving up or down. This procedure reduces average shares in periods of lower securities prices and fewer shares in periods of higher prices.

Dollar-cost averaging—A system of buying securities at regular intervals with a fixed dollar amount. Under the system, the investors buy by dollars' worth rather than by the numbers of shares. If each investment is the same number of dollars' payments, buy more shares when the price is low and less when it increases. Temporary downswings in price thus benefit investors if they continue to make periodic purchases in both good times and bad, and the price at which the shares are sold is more than their average cost.

Domestic company—An insurance company that is incorporated under the laws of the state where it is operating. A life insurance company incorporated in Indiana is known as a domestic insurance carrier in Indiana.

Double taxation—The federal government taxes corporate profits once as corporate income; any part of the remaining profits distributed as dividends to stockholders may be taxed again as income to the recipient.

Dow Jones average—Widely quoted stock averages computed regularly. They include an industrial average, a rail average, a utility average, and a combination of the three.

Dow Jones utility average—The index of utility stocks.

E

Elimination period—The elimination period is a waiting period before benefits are payable under an accident and health policy that proves disability income payments. Policies may contain an elimination (waiting) period of any length but 30 days is quite common.

Emergency access—Emergencies are inevitable. If you fail to plan for emergencies, you will continually dip into your intermediate and long-term assets. Keeping debt under control is essential. This book will help you establish an adequate emergency fund.

Endowment—Life insurance payable to the policyholder if living, on the maturity date stated in the policy, or to a beneficiary if the insured dies prior to the date.

Endowment—A permanent plan of life insurance that makes two promises. If the insured dies during the policy term, the face amount will be payable. If the insured is still living at the end of the endowment period, the face amount is also payable. The endowment policy puts emphasis on savings.

Entire contract—The policy and the attached application is the entire contract of the life or health insurance. Company manuals, rules and underwriting guides can not be incorporated into the policy by reference.

Equity—The ownership in common and preferred stockholders in a company. Also refers to excess of value of securities over the debit balance in a margin account. Also, the value of the property that remains after all liens and other charges against the property are paid. A property owner's equity generally consists of his or her monetary interest in the property in excess of the mortgage indebtedness. In the case of long-term mortgage, the owner's equity builds up quite gradually during the first several years because the bulk of each monthly payment is applied not to the principal amount of the loan, but to the interest.

Equity investments—Owner investments are stock investments, either common or preferred. When you buy a stock you buy a piece of a company.

ERISA—The Employee Retirement Income Security Act. Passed by Congress in 1974 to remedy alleged abuses and insure the safety of pension plans for the worker.

Established growth stocks—Better known, larger growth companies (*i.e.* Walt Disney, Proctor and Gamble).

Exchange privilege—An option enabling mutual fund shareholders to transfer their investment from one fund to another within the same fund family as their needs or objectives change. Typically, funds allow investors to use the exchange privilege several times a year for a low fee per exchange.

Ex-dividend date—When used in reference to mutual funds, the ex-dividend date is the date on which declared distribution (dividends or capital gains) are deducted from the fund's assets before it calculates its net asset value. The NAV per share will drop by the amount of the distribution per share.

Ex-dividend date—The date on which the stock trades without the right to receive the dividend.

Exclusion ratio—The portion of each annuity payment that is excluded from taxes as a return of principal (exclusion allowance).

Expense ratio—A fund's cost of doing business, disclosed in the prospectus as a percent of assets.

Ex-rights—The stock does not trade with the preemptive right.

Extended term—One of the nonforfeiture options. The cash value is used as a single premium to buy the term insurance in the amount of the policy at the insured's age at time of lapse. It is the option that is automatic if the insured does not elect another one.

Extended term insurance—A form of insurance available as a nonforfeiture option. It provides the original amount of insurance for a limited period of time.

F

Face amount—The amount stated on the face of the policy that will be paid in the event of death or at the maturity of the policy.

Fair Credit Reporting Act—An act passed by Congress in 1971 that enables applicants for insurance to clear up any misinformation that may effect their insurability. It requires disclosure of the source of information that the insurance company based their decision on.

Family plans—The name given to life insurance policies that insure all members of the family under one contract. The insured, spouse, children and children born after the policy becomes active are insured. Generally they provide a whole life policy on the insured and term insurance on the spouse and children.

Family of funds—A mutual fund "family" is a number of different investment objectives, managed and distributed by the same company.

Financial planning—The wise use of your assets to help you make maximum use of every before-tax and after-tax dollar.

Fixed amount—This refers to the taking of the policy proceeds in fixed amounts. An example would be to take the life insurance policy proceeds monthly in $500 amounts. The policy will pay until the principal and interest are exhausted.

Fixed annuity—A fixed annuity is a contract with an insurance company which accumulates guaranteed interest on a tax-deferred basis. The interest can be guaranteed for various lengths of time. Once the guaranteed period has expired, the insurance company will declare a new interest rate, typically guaranteed for one year. It should be noted that in a fixed annuity the principal is never at risk. A fixed annuity has characteristics that are similar to a CD.

Fixed period—The payment of the life insurance policy proceeds over a certain period. This period could be 1 year, 10 years or some other period of time. There is a limit on this time, generally 30 years. The longer the period the smaller the amount.

Flexible premium policy—A life insurance policy under which the policyholder or contractholder may vary the amounts or timing of premium payments.

Flexible premium variable life insurance—A life insurance policy that combines the premium flexibility feature of universal life insurance with the equity-based benefit feature of variable life insurance.

Flexible premium—These contracts allow for multiple premium contributions. Much like a mutual fund investment, these contracts will typically require an initial investment of $1000 or more and then will allow subsequent investments for as little as $25 per month depending on the contract.

Floor—The huge trading area of a stock exchange where stocks and bonds are bought and sold.

401(k) plan—An employer-sponsored retirement plan that enables employees to defer taxes on a portion of their salaries by earmarking that portion for the retirement plan.

403(b) plan—An employer-sponsored retirement plan that enables employers of universities, public schools and non-profit organizations to defer taxes on a portion of their salaries by earmarking that portion for the retirement plan.

Foreign insurance company—A company organized under the laws of one state and operating in another. An example would be a Wisconsin life insurance company operating in Illinois. This company would be a foreign life insurance company under the Illinois law. In Wisconsin it would be known as a domestic insurance company.

Fully managed fund—A mutual fund whose investment policy gives its management complete flexibility as to the types of investments made and the proportions of each. Management is restricted only to the extent that federal or blue sky laws require.

Fundamental analysis—The evaluation of companies as to their investment potential based on their financial, competitive and earnings position.

G

General agent—A general agent is appointed to develop and supervise a book of business for an insurance company. The general agent is compensated by commissions on the business that his agent produces. Some general agents personally produce business themselves while others perform only management and administrative duties.

General Obligation Bond (GOB)—A common type of municipal bond. They are backed by the full faith and taxing power of the issuer.

Gilt-edged—High-grade bond issued by a company that has demonstrated its ability to earn a comfortable profit over a period of years and pay its bond-holders interest without interruption.

GNMA and FNMA certificate backed bonds—Nickname for the Government National Mortgage Association and the Federal National Mortgage Association, respectively. Securities are guaranteed by these agencies.

Good 'till canceled (OTC) order—An order to buy or sell securities that remain in effect until executed or canceled.

Government agency bonds—Issued by mortgage associations and backed by governmental agencies but are not a direct obligation of the U.S. government. They are AAA-rated. Ginnie Mae, Fannie Mae, and Freddie Mac are the three most well known.

Government bonds—Obligations of the U.S. Government, regarded as the highest grade issues in existence.

Government securities fund—A mutual fund which purchases securities issued by U.S. Government agencies.

Grace period—A period (usually 30 or 31 days) following the premium date, during which an overdue premium may be paid without penalty. The policy remains in force throughout this period.

Gross premium—The premium which includes the amount needed to pay losses plus the amount that will be used to pay expenses and an allowance for profit.

Gross profit—Reflects a company's markup or its cost of goods sold as well as management's ability to control these costs in relation to sales.

Group insurance—Insurance written to cover a certain number of people. The minimum number of lives is usually 10. Some groups cover many thousands of lives. The insurance benefits under group may provide life and/or accident and health coverage.

Group life insurance—Life insurance usually without medical examination, on a group of people under a master policy. It is typically issued to an employer for the benefits of the employees, or to members of an association. The individual members of the group hold certificates as evidence of their insurance.

Growth fund—A fund comprised of companies whose rate of growth over a period of time is considerably greater than that of businesses generally.

Growth managers—Invest exclusively in growth stocks.

Growth stock—Common stock of a company with a record of relatively rapid earnings growth.

Guaranteed insurability—A contractual provision that allows the insured to purchase additional amounts of insurance for life or accident and health without having to submit to the insurance company any evidence of insurability. The policy will grant these options to buy additional insurance at set intervals.

Guaranteed interest rate—The absolute minimum that the insurance company will ever pay on both new contributions, as well as existing monies in the contract.

H

Health Maintenance Organization (HMO)—An organization that contracts with providers of medical services (physicians and hospitals) to provide medical services to the members of HMO.

Health insurance—Often called accident and health insurance. This is the insurance that protects us against loss of income, medical expenses, hospital costs, accidental death and dismemberment and skilled nursing home care.

Hospital expenses—Refers to the hospital room, board and regular nursing charges for in-patient confinement. Usually defined to include medical and surgical services and supplies provided by the hospital.

HR-10 or Keogh plan—An act passed by congress that allows anyone who pays self-employed social security taxes to establish a retirement plan with tax deductible contributions.

I

Ibbotson charts—Plot the historic return on treasury bills, treasury bonds, large-cap stocks found in the S&P 500, small-cap stocks, and inflation. It generally goes back to 1926.

Income for a specified period—A monthly check for a selected period of time.

Income of a specified amount—A monthly check for a selected amount.

Income dividends—Payments to mutual fund shareholders of dividends, interest, and/or short-term capital gains earned on the fund's portfolio securities after deducting operating expenses.

Income fund—A mutual fund with a primary objective of current income.

Income stocks—A common stock of a company that pays large, regular dividends.

Incontestable clause—A provision in the life policy that forbids the insurance company from contesting any statements of the insured on the application after passage of time, usually 2 years. In health insurance policies it is often called "time limit on certain defenses."

Indemnity—The payment of an insurance benefit so that the insured does not profit from the loss. Life insurance policies are not contracts of indemnity. Most accident and health policies are contracts of indemnity and the payments under these policies are limited to the actual payments made by the insured.

Individual Retirement Account (IRA)—A personal tax sheltered retirement plan that is available to any wage earner who is not currently participating in any other plan.

Individual Retirement Account (IRA)—An investor-established account set up to hold funds until retirement.

Industrial insurance—Insurance that is issued in small amounts and the premium is collected by the agent at the home or place of work of the insured.

Inflation risk—Chance that the value of assets or of income will be eroded as inflation shrinks the value of a country's currency.

Immediate annuity—An annuity contract that will begin paying benefits immediately.

Inspection report—The name given to the report filed with the insurance company by a company that has made an inspection report on the insured. The material reported usually deals with employment, lifestyle, and hobbies of the insured.

Insurability—Acceptability of the company of an applicant for insurance.

Insurance examiner—The representative of a state insurance department assigned to participate in the official audit and examination of the affairs of an insurance company.

Insured or insured life—The person on whose life the policy is insured.

Insurance—A social device for transferring the risk of death or poor health along with the funds, known as the premium, which are accumulated for the payment of future losses.

Insurance policy—In daily use the printed and typed (can be hand written) document that the insured receives which describes the coverage purchased.

Insurable interest—An interest in a person's continued life or good health that can be measured monetarily. Certain close relationships (marriage for example) automatically gives rise to an insurable interest. A person is said to have an unlimited insurable interest in their own life.

Insuring clause—The promise in life insurance is to pay to the designated beneficiary. This beneficiary has rights and his/her consent is needed for policy changes.

Irrevocable beneficiary—A beneficiary that can't be changed without the consent of the irrevocable beneficiary. This beneficiary has rights and his/her consent is needed for policy changes.

Interest rate risk—The uncertainty of returns on investments due to change in market rates of interest.

International managers—Invest primarily in American Depository Receipts (ADRs) of foreign corporations. They can be either value or growth style managers.

Investor—An individual whose principal concerns in the purchase of a security are regular dividend income and/or capital appreciation without unnecessary risk.

Investment company—A corporation, trust, or partnership that invests pooled funds of shareholders in securities appropriate to the fund's objective. Among the benefits of investment companies, compared to direct investments, are professional management and diversification. Mutual Funds (also known as "open-ended" investment companies) are the most popular type of investment company.

Investment objective—The goal—*e.g.*, long-term capital growth, current income, etc.—that the investor and mutual fund pursue together.

J

The January Effect—Phenomenon that stocks (especially small stocks) have historically tended to rise markedly during the period starting on the last day of December and ending the fourth trading day of January.

Joint and last survivor—One monthly check for as long as the annuitant and a secondary payee are living. The surviving payee will continue to receive the payments for an equal or an adjusted amount as originally directed for life.

Joint life—The insuring of two lives under a single policy.

Joint life annuity—An annuity whose payments are made to more than one (usually two) person. Often referred to as joint and survivorship.

K

Keogh plan—The HR-10. The retirement plan for the self-employed.

Key man insurance—Today referred to as insurance on the key person. Business often recognizes the particular contributions of certain people to the firm. The cost of hiring and training replacement upon the death of the key person can be substantial and key man insurance fills the need.

L

Laddered portfolio—An effective bond strategy that uses staggering maturities so that one has a bond maturing every year for ten years. Every year, as one instrument matures, you would purchase another maturing in ten years.

Lapse policy—A policy terminated for non-payment of premiums. The term is sometimes limited to the termination occurring before the policy has a crash or surrender value.

Legal reserve life insurance policy—A life insurance company operating under state insurance laws specifying the minimum basis for the reserves the company must maintain on its policies.

Leverage—The use of debt or securities such as options and warrants to increase potential returns.

Loan value—Permanent life insurance policies that have been in force for a certain period of time build up what is known as a cash value. This cash value can be borrowed by the owner of the policy at any time at an interest rate that is stated in the policy.

Long-term funds—An industry designation for all the funds other than short-term funds (taxable and tax-exempt money market funds). Long-term funds are broadly divided into equity (stock) and bonds and income funds.

Lump sum—The amount of insurance that is payable upon the death of an insured or upon the insured suffering dismemberment as defined in the policy. Taking the proceeds in cash, instead of under a settlement option, is often called a lump sum settlement.

M

Major medical—An accident and health policy that is designed to pay the large medical expense bills that can be incurred by an insured. The policy has a deductible, a method of sharing the cost which is called coinsurance, and a high total limit of liability.

Management fee—The amount paid by a mutual fund to the investor adviser for its services. The average annual fee industry wide is about one half of one percent of fund assets.

Market order—An order to buy or sell a security at the best available price.

Market risk—Uncertainty over the movement of market prices of securities.

Market timing—Active management of stocks that entails shifting funds between stocks and money market securities as economic conditions change.

Master contract—The policy between the insurance company and policyholder that grants the group insurance coverage.

Master policy—A policy that is issued to an employer or trustee, establishing a group insurance plan for designated members of an eligible group.

Medicaid—A program to help people who cannot afford health care. It includes their dependents. The federal government pays part of the cost and the states provide the administrative.

Medicare—That part of the social security program that provides hospital and surgical insurance to those over 65 and certain others that qualify.

Medical application—An application for insurance that requires the taking of a physical examination, either by a doctor or other medical professional.

Medical expense—The term used to describe the expenses of an illness from hospital, doctors, drugs and other medical services and supplies.

Medical Information Bureau (MIB)—An organization that maintains medical information files on applicants for life and health insurance.

Minimizing taxes—Taxes have a massive impact on your net spendable income. Understanding what taxes are today and what they are likely to be in the future is critical. You will learn six tax reduction strategies.

Misrepresentation—An untrue statement made by the applicant who is applying for insurance. Also to apply to statements by the agent that are not truthful about the terms and coverage of the insurance being presented.

Misstatement of age—A provision in the life insurance policy that adjusts the benefits to what the premium would have purchased at the correct age of the insured.

Miscellaneous hospital expense—The changes made by a hospital for other than room, board and regular nursing.

Mode of premium—The frequency of premium payment—annual, semi-annual, quarterly or monthly.

Modified whole life—A whole life insurance policy that has a lower premium during the first couple of years. Enables the person to buy whole life now at a premium that will be lower now but will increase at a later date.

Money managers—Are investment advisors with highly specialized styles and investment philosophies. They fashion their style after a particular stock or bond class. Managers are either fixed income managers (bonds) or equity managers (stock) or combination of the two (balanced).

Money market funds—Open-ended mutual fund that invests in commercial paper, banker's acceptances, repurchase agreements, government securities, certificates of deposit, and other highly liquid and safe securities.

Monetary pressure index—Determines the market environment for both stocks and bonds. Removes the bond from the books and enables the municipality to sell more bonds. When a bond is pre-refunded, the call date becomes the maturity date and the rating becomes AAA. These are the safest form of municipal investments.

Morbidity—Poor health, sickness. The morbidity tables give the rate of disability from illness.

Mortality table—A statistical table showing the death rate at each age, usually expressed as so many (deaths) per thousand.

Municipal bond—A bond issued by a state or a political subdivision such as a county, city, town, or village. The term also designates bonds issued by state agencies and authorities. Generally, interest paid on municipal bonds is exempt from federal income taxes and from state and local income taxes within the state issue.

Municipal notes—Have a maturity ranging from three months to three years and are issued to raise money for temporary financing of capital improvements or to even cash flows of municipalities.

Mutual fund—An investment company that pools money from shareholders and invests in a variety of securities, including stocks, bonds, and money market instruments. A mutual fund stands ready to buy back (redeem) its shares at their current net asset value; this value depends on the market value of the fund's portfolio securities at the time of redemption.

Mutual insurance company—A corporation that is organized to carry on the business of insurance. The policyholders own the insurance company.

N

NASD—The National Association of Securities Dealers, Inc. An association of brokers and dealers in the over-the-counter securities business. The association has the power to expel members who have been declared guilty of unethical practices. The NASD is dedicated, among other objectives, "to adopt, administer and enforce rules of fair practice and rules to prevent fraudulent and manipulative acts and practices, and in general to promote just and equitable principals of trade for the protection of investors."

Net asset value per share—The market worth of one share of a mutual fund. This figure is derived by taking a fund's total assets—securities, cash, and any accrued earnings—deducting liabilities, and dividing by the number of shares outstanding.

Net premium—That part of the premium that is used to pay the losses. There is no part of this premium used to pay the expenses of writing and keeping the policy in force.

New issue—A stock or bond sold by a corporation for the first time. Proceeds may be issued to retire outstanding securities of the company, for new plant or equipment, or for additional working capital.

Noncancellable—A policy that cannot be canceled by the insurance company. Often used to describe the noncancellable and guaranteed renewable disability income policy.

Nonforfeiture values—After a certain period of time, permanent life insurance policies have a value that will not be forfeited by the insured if the policy lapses. These values are cash surrender, reduced paid-up and extended term.

No-load fund—A mutual fund selling its shares at net asset value without any sales charges.

Non-medical—Insurance issued on an application that has not required the applicant to take a physical examination.

Non-medical limit—The maximum face value of a policy that a given company will issue without the applicant taking a medical examination.

Non-participating policy—A life insurance policy in which the company does not distribute to policyholders any part of its surplus.

Non-occupational—A policy that does not cover sickness or accident that arises out of and in the course of the insured's employment.

Non-solicited—The client calls a broker to execute a stock trade with no consultation from the broker. (Also called unsolicited.)

O

OASDHI—Old age, survivors, disability and health insurance. The social security act.

Odd lot—Less than 100 shares of stock.

Open account—When referring to a mutual fund, a type of account in which the investor may add or withdrawal shares at any time. In such an account, dividends may be paid in cash or reinvested at the account holder's option.

Open-end investment company—An investment company that has outstanding redeemable shares. Also generally applied to those investment companies which continuously offer new shares to the public and stand ready at any time to redeem their outstanding shares.

Open-end mutual fund—Issue shares on a continuing basis. The number of shares increases as money comes into the fund and decreases as shares are redeemed.

Operating expenses—The normal costs a mutual fund incurs in conducting business, such as the expenses associated with maintaining offices, staff, and equipment. There are also expenses related to maintaining the fund's portfolio of securities. These expenses are paid from the fund's assets before any earnings are distributed to shareholders.

Open order—An order that remains in effect until it is either executed or canceled by the investor.

Opening price—The first trade price of the day for a security.

Operating profit—Shows the profitability of a company on its normal course of operations and provides a measure of the operating efficiency of the company.

Over-the-counter—Stocks that are traded amongst dealers either by telephone or electronically for retail clients as opposed to an exchange floor.

Owner—The person who is in control of the insurance policy. In the vast majority of cases the owner is also the insured.

P

Paid-up insurance—Insurance on which all required premiums have been paid.

Participating policy—A life insurance policy under which the company agrees to distribute to the policyholders the part of its surplus which its Board of Directors determines is not needed at the end of the business year. Such a distribution serves to reduce the premium the policyholder has been paid.

Participating preferred stock—A preferred stock that pays a fixed dividend and participates in any additional earnings that may be distributed to common shareholders.

Payment date—Date on which dividends are paid to investors on record.

Payout ratio—The percentage of the company's earnings paid in dividends to shareholders.

Payor benefit—Used in juvenile policies to insure the life of the premium payor until the insured reaches a particular age. If the premium payor dies, the insurance company will make the premium payments until the juvenile insured reaches the age stated in the policy, such as age 21.

Pension plan—A plan that will pay an income at retirement to the insured.

Performance—A measure of how well your investment is doing; yield and total return are two commonly used mutual fund performance measures.

Permanent life insurance—A phrase used to cover any form of life insurance except term; generally insurance that accrues cash value, such as whole life endowment.

Pink sheets—The daily published listing of some of the thinly traded over-the-counter stocks.

Policy—The printed legal document stating the terms of the insurance contract that is issued to the policy holder by the company.

Policyholder—The person who owns a life insurance policy. This is usually the insured person, but may also be a relative of the insured, a partnership or a corporation.

Policy loan—A loan made by a life insurance company from its general funds to policyholder on the security of the cash value of a policy.

Policy reserves—The measure of the funds that a life insurance company holds specifically for fulfillment of its policy obligations. Reserves are required by law to be so calculated that, together with future earnings, they will enable the company to pay all future claims.

Pooling—Pooling is the basic concept behind mutual funds. A fund pools the money of thousand of individual and institutional investors who share common financial goals. The fund uses this pool to buy a diversified portfolio of investments. Each mutual fund share purchased represents ownership in all the fund's underlying securities.

Portfolio—A collection of securities owned by an individual or an institution (such as a mutual fund). A fund's portfolio may include a combination of stocks, bonds, and money market securities.

Portfolio turnover—A measure in the trading activity in the fund's portfolio of investments: how often securities are bought and sold by the fund.

Preexisting conditions—Health conditions that were in existence at the time the policy was effective. Individual and group accident and health policies treat them in a variety of ways, from full coverage, to elimination for a set time period, to excluding the condition specifically by name.

Preemptive right—The right of common shareholders to buy new shares before they are offered to other investors.

Preferred stock—A class stock with claim on the company's earnings before payment may be made on common stock and usually entitled a priority over common stock if the company liquidates. Usually entitled to dividends at a specified rate, when declared by the board of directors and before payment of a dividend on the common stock, depending on the term of issue.

Premium—The payment, or one of the periodic payments, a policyholder agrees to make for an insurance policy.

Premium loan—A policy loan made for the purpose for paying premiums.

Prerefunded bonds—Are callable, but at some time before the call date arrives, the municipality backs the bonds with U.S. treasuries. A city or municipality has a limit to the amount of debt it can have on its books, so when a municipality pre-refunds a bond, it will raise taxes without limit to repay you.

Price-earnings ratio—The price of a share of stock divided by earnings per share for a twelve-month period. For example, a stock selling for $100 a share and earning $5 a share is said to be selling at a price-earnings ratio of 20 to 1.

Price/earning ratio (P/E)—A measure of the number of times that a stock's price exceeds its earnings.

Primary beneficiary—The beneficiary who will receive the insurance proceeds upon the death of the insured. The beneficiary is named first.

Principal—The initial amount of money you invest.

Probationary period—A period of time in an accident and health contract, individual or group, that excludes sickness contracted or first manifesting itself during that period.

Professional management—The pool of shareholder dollars invested in a mutual fund is managed by full-time, experienced professionals who decide which securities to hold, when to buy, and when to sell.

Prospectus—The official document that describes a mutual fund and must be furnished to all investors. It contains information required by the Securities and Exchange Commission on such subjects as the fund's investment objectives, policies, services, and fees. A more detailed document, known as "part B" of the registration statement or the "Statement of Additional Information," is available at no charge upon request.

Put—An option to sell a specified number of shares at a definite price within a specified period of time. The opposite of a call.

Purchasing power risk—The uncertainty associated with inflation.

R

Rally—A brisk rise following a decline in the general market or in an individual stock

Rated policy—A policy that has had the premium increased to compensate for the increased mortality or morbidity that the underwriter feels is present in the insured.

Rebating—The return of a portion of the premium, or giving something else of value, to the insured. This result is the insured paying less than other risks in the same category. It is an illegal practice and state insurance laws and regulations provide various penalties for any agent who engages in the practice.

Recurrent disability—A disability that results from or is contributed to by any cause which is the same or related to any cause of any prior period of disability.

Record date—The date on which a shareholder must be a registered owner in order to receive dividends declared by the company.

Redeem—To cash in your shares by selling them back to the mutual fund. Mutual fund shares may be redeemed on any business day.

Redemption price—The amount per share (shown as the "bid" in newspaper tables) that mutual fund shareholders receive when they cash in shares. The value of the shares depends on the market value of the fund's portfolio securities at the time. This value is the same as "net asset value per share."

Red herring—A preliminary used to obtain indications of interest from prospective buyers of a new issue.

Reduced paid-up insurance—A form of insurance available as a nonforfeiture option. It provides for the continuation of the original insurance plan, but for a reduced amount.

Reduced paid-up—One of the nonforfeiture options. Allows the insured to have a completely paid-up policy of the same type for a lesser amount upon policy lapse.

Reinstatement—The policy provision that allows the insured to apply for reinstatement of his or her lapsed policy within a three or five year period after the date of lapse. The provision spells out the requirements for reinstatement.

Reinvestment privilege—An option available to mutual fund shareholders in which fund dividends and capital gain distributions are automatically turned back into the fund to buy new shares and thus increasing holdings.

Related policy—Sometimes called an "extra-risk" policy, an insurance policy issued at a higher-than-standard-premium rate to cover the extra risk where, for example, an insured has impaired health or a hazardous occupation.

Renewability-health insurance—The right to renew the policy. Is it conditional, or is it guaranteed? The insured's right to continue the contract of health insurance and under what conditions, along with the insurance company's right to renew or not renew, is the subject of renewability.

Renewable term insurance—Term insurance which can be renewed at the end of the term, at the option of the policyholder and without evidence of insurability, for a limited number of successive terms. The rates increase at each renewal as the age of the insured increases.

Renewable term—The statements made by the insured to induce the insurance company to issue an insurance policy. In life insurance, these statements are entered on the application and made a part of the insurance policy.

Renewal interest rate—The interest rate declared by the insurance company after the initial guaranteed rate period has elapsed. The renewal rate will typically be guaranteed by the insurance company for one year.

Representation—The statement made by the insured to induce the insurance company to issue an insurance policy. In life insurance, these statements are entered on the application and made a part of the insurance policy.

Reserve—The amount required to be carried as a liability in the financial statement of the insurer, to be provide for future commitments under policies outstanding.

Retirement planning—Retirement should be a time when you have more, not fewer options. Retirement and other financial goals usually involve a long-term holding period or investment span. This book will help you to put distractions that change constantly, like current investment earnings, in perspective and teach you to focus on performance consistent with your investment span.

Return—The dividends or interest paid by a company expressed as a percentage of the current price. A stock with a current market value of $20 a share that has paid $1 in dividends in the preceding twelve months is said to return 5 percent ($1.00/$20.00). The current return on a bond is figured the same way. Another term for yield.

Return on common equity—This ratio indicates how well management is performing for the stockholders.

Revenue bonds—Another type of municipal bond. They are backed by a specific revenue source instead of the full taxing power of the municipality.

Rider—A special policy provision or group of provisions that may be added to a policy to expand or limit the benefits otherwise payable.

Rider—The attachment to the policy of a form that adds amounts, limits coverage, or broadens coverage is called a rider.

Right—An option issued to shareholders that allow them to buy a specified number of the company's new shares at a subscription price.

Risk—Risk refers to the variability of value. In investing, risk can be credit risk, principal risk, inflation risk, or interest rate risk, to name a few. The type of risk incurred by a shareholder varies from fund to fund. An investor will often tolerate higher levels of risk in return for potentially higher monetary rewards.

Risk/reward tradeoff—A basic investment principal that holds that an investment principal for increasing returns (higher earnings) in order to compensate for increasing levels of risk. This tradeoff reflects the investor's willingness to accept gains and losses—change, uncertainty, volatility—in the short run for the prospect of net gain in the long run that's larger than gains associated with absolute stability.

Risk classification—The process by which a company decides how its premium rates for life insurance should differ according to the risk characteristics of the individuals insured (*e.g.*, age, occupation, sex, state of health) and then applies the resulting rules to individual applications. (see: Underwriting.)

Round lot—One hundred shares of stock in multiples of 100.

Rule of 72—The rule of 72 allows investors to determine the number of years required to double your investment at a given rate of return. For example, 72 divided by the rate of return (example $72 \div 15$) = 4.8 years, the number of years to double your investment.

S

Sales charge—An amount charged to purchase shares in many mutual funds sold by brokers or other sales agents. The maximum charge is 8.5 percent of the initial investment. The charge is added to the net asset value per share when determining the offer price.

SAR-SEP—Salary deferred simplified employee pension plan is a variation on a SEP plan. The maximum investment is $9,240 per year or up to 15 percent of the eligible payroll. Employers may contribute to the plan, but these contributions are counted toward the 15 percent limit. This investment is made with pre-tax dollars and is deferred until withdrawal.

Seat—A traditional figure of speech for a membership on an exchange. Price and admission requirements vary.

Secondary payee—The individual who will continue to receive monthly benefits under a joint and last survivor payout option.

Sector rotation managers—Do less stock picking. They are more concerned with being in the right industry at the right time.

Securities and Exchange Commission (SEC)—The Securities and Exchange Commission is the federal agency that regulates registration and distribution of mutual fund shares.

SEP—Or Simplified Employee Pension plan, is for a person who is self-employed with no employees or self-employed with employees. Employees do not contribute personally to a SEP program—it is solely employer funded.

Separate account—An asset account established by a life insurance company separate from other funds, used primarily for pension plans and variable life products.

Series funds—Funds that are organized with separate portfolios of securities, each with its own investment objective.

Settlement options—The several ways, other than immediate payment in cash, which a policyholder or beneficiary may choose to have policy benefits paid.

Shareholder—An investor; the owner of shares of a mutual fund or the owner of shares of corporate stock.

Short-term funds—An industry designation for funds that invest primarily in securities with maturities less than one year. Short-term funds include taxable money market funds (also known as short-term municipal bond funds).

Single Premium Deferred Annuity or SPDA—A single premium deferred annuity is a fixed annuity that is funded with a single premium contribution. No subsequent contributions may be made.

Solicited—The broker calls the client to suggest a stock for their portfolio.

Sound principals—A sound principal is a fundamental rule that will stand the test of time. Diversifying your portfolio and systematically saving are two examples of sound principals. Other sound principals are discussed throughout this book.

Split—The division of the outstanding shares of a corporation into a larger number of shares. A 3-for-1 split by a company with 1 million shares outstanding results in 3 million shares outstanding. Each holder of 100 shares before the 3-to-1 split would have 300 shares, although the proportionate equity in the company would remain the same; 100 parts of 1 million are the equivalent of 300 parts of 3 million.

Special situation—Buying for a specific, expected result and fundamental change such as a takeover. This is an example of value investing.

Spread—The difference between the bid price and the offering price. Also, the combination of a put and a call "points away" from the market.

Spread—The difference between the bid and asked price of a security.

S&P 500 Index—A composite of 500 companies representing an industry-wide sample of the entire actively-traded U.S. equities market; it contains industrial, utility, financial, and transportation stocks. Unlike the DJIA, the 500 also contains NASDAQ and American Stock Exchange issues.

Statement of Additional Information (SAI)—This document, also known as "Part B" of the registration statement, contains more detailed, supplementary information about a mutual fund. It is available upon request at no charge from the fund.

Stock—An investment that represents a share of ownership in a corporation. The performance of the corporation will influence the value of the stock.

Stock certificate—A certificate that provides physical evidence of stock ownership.

Stock dividend—Dividends paid to shareholders in the form of additional shares of the company's stock.

Stock dividend—A dividend paid in securities rather than cash. The dividend may be additional shares of the issuing company or shares of another company (usually a subsidiary) held by the issuing company.

Stock exchange—An organization registered under the Securities Exchange Act of 1934 with physical facilities for the buying and selling of securities in a two-way auction.

Stock fund—Mutual fund which invests in common and preferred stocks and *NO* bonds.

Stock insurance company—An insurance company that is owned by its stock-holders.

Stock market exchange—A place where buyers and sellers of stocks execute their trades; the most recognized are the New York Stock Exchange (NYSE), American Stock Exchange (AMEX) and an electronic exchange for over-the-counter securities, National Association of Securities Dealers Automation Quotations (NASDAQ).

Stock quotes—The bid and ask (offer) price for a stock; bid—the price you will receive for a stock; ask (offer)—the price you will pay to buy the stock.

Stock split—When a company increases the number of shares outstanding by exchanging a specified number of new shares for each existing share.

Stop limit order—A trading order that specifies both a limit price and a stock price. When the price of a security reaches the stop price, a limit order is created at the limit price.

Stop loss—The point where you want to sell your stock. It can be entered at the time of purchase. If your stock drops to your "stop," it will automatically be sold. Stops remove the emotion involved in selling stock.

Stop order—A trading order that specifies a stop price. When the security reaches the stop price, a market order is created.

Suicide clause—The provision in the life insurance policy that excludes suicide from coverage under the policy during the first two years of the policy.

Straight life insurance—Whole life insurance on which premiums are payable for life.

Suitability rate—The rule of fair practice that requires a member to have reasonable grounds for believing that a recommendation to a customer is suitable on the basis of the customer's financial objectives and abilities.

Surgical expense—The accident and health policy benefit that provides coverage for the physician's charge for surgical procedures.

Surrender charge—Most annuity contracts, both fixed and variable, have no front-end sales charges. However, they will charge a penalty for early withdrawal much like a CD. This penalty is necessary in order to keep the investor in the contract long enough for the insurance company to recoup the cost of placing the contract. The surrender charge will typically be placed on a sliding scale so that the longer the investor is in the contract, the lower the surrender charge. Eventually, the charge will decline to zero.

Surrender value—The surrender value of an annuity contract is the accumulated cash value, less any surrender penalties that remain in the contract.

Tax-deferred or deferred annuity—All earnings will accumulate tax-deferred in the contract until withdrawn from the contract.

Tax-exempt bond—Free from federal tax liability. This is granted to municipal bonds.

Ten-day free look—Allows the insured to examine the policy for 10 days and if not completely satisfied return the policy to the agent or company for a full refund of the premium paid. A requirement in some states.

Technical analysis—A method of evaluating securities using past price and volume data.

Technical analysis—A chart of a stock's performance based on supply and demand.

Tenants in common—A form of registration of property, frequently used with securities. An undivided estate in property where, upon the death of the owner, the undivided estate becomes the property of heirs or devisees and not of the surviving co-owner.

Term insurance—Life insurance payable to a beneficiary only when an insured dies within a specified period.

Term life insurance—A life insurance policy that pays only if the insured dies during the term coverage. The term policy gives protection only, and it expires without value at the end of the term.

Third market—A secondary security market where exchange-listed stocks trade on the over-the-counter.

Top-down approach—The preferred approach for buying and selling stocks. One first examines the economy to determine its stage—whether it is in a recession, early stage recovery, late stage recovery, or expansion. Next look at stocks that do well in the current stage.

Total disability—A condition that must be met under a disability income policy in order for the policy to pay income benefits to the insured. It is defined differently in different policies. The liberal definition is the inability to perform the insured's occupation and is usually restricted to the early years of disability. Inability to engage in an occupation for which the insured is reasonably suited by education and training is the most common definition to be met for continued disability. The inability to engage in any occupation for wage or profit is the most restrictive definition.

Total return—A measure of an investment's performance that takes into account all three components of earnings per share: dividends, capital gains distribution, and price appreciation.

Transfer agent—The organization employed by a mutual fund to prepare and maintain records relating to the accounts of its shareholders. Some funds serve as their own transfer agents.

Treasury bill—Short-term government bonds issued in $1,000 units with maturity or longer than five years. They are traded on the market like other bonds.

Treasury note—Intermediate-term government paper, with maturities ranging from one to five years.

Treasury stock—Outstanding stock that is repurchased by the issuing company.

Turnaround—Refers to a company that is restructuring debt or restricting management. This stock is considered value investing.

12b-1 fee—The fee named for the SEC rule changed by some funds to pay for distribution costs, such as advertising and dealer compensation. The fund's prospectus outlines 12b-1 fees, if applicable.

U

Uptick—A trade in a security that is made at a higher price than the previous trade.

Underwriting—The process by which a life insurance company determines whether or not it can accept an application for life insurance, and if so, on what basis.

Unlisted stock—Stocks not listed on the exchanges.

Universal life insurance—A flexible premium life insurance policy under which the policyholder may change the death benefit from time to time (with satisfactory evidence of insurability for increases) and vary the amount or timing of premium payments. Premiums (less expense charge) are credited to a policy account from which mortality charges are deducted and to which interest is credited at rates which may change from time to time.

Unsystematic risk—The risk of a security that does not relate to the market and can be diversified away.

V

Valuation—Determines whether the market is historically high or low. Look at price-to-dividends ratios, price-to-earnings ratios, and price-to-book values.

Value investing—Investing in companies in order to buy low and sell higher, because those companies are perceived to be unloved or out of favor.

Value managers—Invest in stock they consider to be undervalued.

Value stocks—Generally above-average yield stocks and/or unusually low P/E and or low price to asset value.

Vanish premium—A premium payment option the client may choose whereby dividends earned are applied to reduce the annual premium. Whether the premium will "vanish" depends on actual experiences and dividends paid by the insurance carrier.

Variable annuity—An investment contract sold to an investor by an insurance company. Capital is accumulated, often through investment in a mutual fund, and converted to an income stream at a future date, often retirement. Income payments vary with the value of the account.

Variable life insurance—Life insurance under which the benefits relate to the value of assets behind the contract at the time the benefit is paid.

Volatility—The amount by which the price of a security rises or falls during a time period.

Volume—The number of shares of stock traded over a period of time.

W

Waiting period—Same as an elimination period. The period of the time that must pass before the insured will receive disability income payments.

Waiver—The voluntary surrendering of a given right. Agents and other company employees might give up a right of the company through their actions.

Waiver of premium—The agreement to waive the premiums during a period of total disability of the insured.